Who is This 'We'?

For those who recognise that presence is not to be trusted.

Who is This 'We'?

Absence of Community

edited by
Eleanor M. Godway and Geraldine Finn

**BLACK
ROSE
BOOKS**

Montréal/New York
London

BLACK ROSE BOOKS No. X211
Hardcover ISBN 1-551640-05-8
Paperback ISBN 1-551640-04-X

Library of Congress No. 94-71247

Canadian Cataloguing in Publication Data

Main entry under title:
Who is this 'we'? : absence of community
Includes bibliographical references.

ISBN 1-551640-05-8 (bound)
ISBN 1-551640-04-X (pbk.)

1. Social ethics. I. Godway, Eleanor M.
II. Finn, Geraldine

HM131.W46 1994   172'.1   C94-900191-0

Photo of Rick Harp's *Certificate of Indian Status*, André Bellefeuille, 1994.

"A Litany for Survival" was reprinted from *The Black Unicorn* by Audre Lorde, with the kind permission of W.W. Norton and Company Inc. Copyright © 1978 by Audre Lorde.

"Into the Midst of It" by Bronwen Wallace is reprinted from *Common Magic*, by permission of Oberon Press.

Mailing Address

BLACK ROSE BOOKS
C.P. 1258
Succ. Place du Parc
Montréal, Québec
H2W 2R3 Canada

BLACK ROSE BOOKS
340 Nagel Drive
Cheektowaga, New York
14225 USA

Printed in Canada
A publication of the Institute of Policy Alternatives of Montréal
(IPAM)

Contents

Acknowledgements

Anna Antonopolous, Karim Benammar, Eleanor Godway, and Barendt Kiefte presented earlier versions of their essays at the annual meeting of the Canadian Society for Hermeneutics and Postmodern Thought, at Carlton University, Ottawa, Canada, in June 1993, where we first had the idea for this book. We would like to thank them and all the contributors for their prompt and enthusiastic response to the idea, and extend a special thank you to Jayne Brewer, Sonja Embree, and our editor at Black Rose Books, Nat Klym, for their help with the preparation of the manuscript.

We would also like to acknowledge our debt to Jacques Derrida and Gayatri Chakravorti Spivak who are a constant inspiration to both of us.

Contributors

Eleanor M. Godway is associate professor of philosophy at Central Connecticut State University. She has published articles on continental philosophy and has edited an issue of *Listening: A Journal of Religion and Culture,* on "Crisis of Faith in the Western World." Her current project is a book on the emergence of meaning as it relates to Merleau-Ponty's notion of "primary speech."

Geraldine Finn is associate professor of cultural studies in the Faculty of Arts at Carleton University. She is co-editor (with Angela Miles) of *Feminism: From Pressure to Politics* (Black Rose Books), editor of *Limited Edition: Voices of Women, Voices of Feminism,* (Fernwood Books), and author of *Why Althusser Killed his Wife: Essays on Discourse and Violence* (forthcoming, Humanities Press).

Anna Antonopoulos has a Ph.D. in humanities from Concordia University, Montréal and teaches in the départment d'études at the Université du Québec à Montréal. She has published articles in various journals and in the anthology *Feminism and the Body* (forthcoming, Indiana University Press). She is currently "scholar in residence" at the University of Calgary where she is working on her book *Space, Gender, Discourse: (De)constructing the 'Home.'*

Karim Benammar received his Ph.D in philosophy from Penn State University in 1993. He is currently studying contemporary Japanese philosophy at Kyoto University.

Sonja Embree lives in Ottawa. She has a B.A. in anthropology and women's studies, and will be entering graduate school in the fall to concentrate on psychoanalytic theory.

Rick Harp has a B.A. in political science and is currently working in Toronto as a producer for CBC's "As it Happens." His interests include the discourse of aboriginality in relation to Canadian politics and the role and function of art as an agent of political change.

Donna Jowett teaches women's studies at the University of Ottawa. She is in the final stages of writing her book *Why Bother Knowing: Ethics, Hermeneutics and the Margins of Women's Studies.*

Barend Kiefte has a B.A. (honours) in philosophy and an M.A. from Memorial University, St. John's, Newfoundland and is currently a Ph.D. candidate at McMaster University. he is interested in Nietzsche and the French postmodernists, especially Foucault and Deleuze.

Christopher Lind has served as Professor of Church and Society at St. Andrew's College, Saskatoon, since 1985. His special areas of interest include ethics and economics, contextual theology, and economic and social justice. He is co-editor of *Coalitions for Justice,* Novalis, Ottawa, 1994 and author of *The Moral Economy of the Farm Crisis: Globalization, and Community,* (forthcoming).

Howard Richards is the author of *The Evaluation of Cultural Action; Etica y Economia; La Ciencia Social al Servicio de la Esperanza,* and other works. He teaches philosophy and in the Peace and Justice Program at Earlham College, and practices law in Santa Barbara.

Introduction

Community: Catachresis: Co~~mmu~~nity

Eleanor M. Godway and Geraldine Finn

Why do we question community and write it as ~~community~~, under
erasure? Surely community refers to something good, that we want to
be part of, that we miss or yearn for, that we at times claim to belong to,
contribute to, and experience as a benediction, where we can be most
fully ourselves? Something which people of good will strive for and
long to bring about? According to John Macmurray, cited by Christopher Lind in chapter 7, "When the System Farms the Farmers," the
answer to the question "is this a community?" is not a matter of fact but
of intention. [1] It is up to us to make community: to find it, build it, or encourage it to grow in our fragmented world. But can we? Or should we
even try, when in spite of good intentions, the effects of community are
often more divisive, more exclusive, and more oppressive, than the absence of community it originally intended to remedy or remove?

We offer this collection as a response to these questions, and the
failure of community as both a theoretical and practical ideal. One
way to symbolize this failure is to write ~~community~~ crossed out, to
alert us to the violences we have experienced in its name and which
we are in danger of reproducing when we assume we already know
what community is, what it looks like, and what is necessary to bring
it about. That is, we write ~~community~~ to alert us to the possibility that
by invoking it by name, we may in fact render the existence of the
community we desire, impossible. Like other words which seem to
defeat themselves, community may have to be understood as a
catachresis in the sense given to the term by Gayatri Spivak. [2]

Catachresis means that there is no literal referent for a particular word; that its definition comes apart, as it were, as soon as we begin to articulate it. This deconstructive awareness of the play of signification does not empty our language of meaning, but rather precipitates us into a crisis of value which calls for an increased circumspection about values, and responsibility for what is done and said in their name. We can neither say what we mean ("community," like "love," has become debased currency), nor mean what we say (that would cost more than we seem to have.) We can only refer to community (or love) in the sense of acknowledging the inadequacy of any of its realizations. But this is not a reason for remaining silent or doing nothing about community. Confronting the crisis of value and assuming responsibility for it means dropping our taken-for-granted assumptions about it; about what we are and what we are doing when we seek community; and inhabiting the aporia this opens up (or, as the phenomenologists would describe it, the *epoche* or the reduction) wherein the task of living, thinking, and being together as a community is experienced as both impossible and essential. These words — living, thinking, and being together — can also be heard as catachreses. And the aporias that they signal are addressed in various ways by the essays which follow; each of which proposes in its own particular way that we experience the abyss — the aporia — which the failure of community has uncovered, and find the courage to let it educate us.

In The Post-Colonial Critic,[3] Spivak uses the term "crisis management" to refer to the problem-solving dynamic of institutions whose overriding logic is protection of the status quo. We can see this, and decry it, as it works against us in bureaucracies and in the economic, political, world-industrial systems, etc. But the logic of crisis management is also true of intellectual institutions — universities, disciplines or orthodoxies, as well as other cultural formations like the Church or the Arts which have an investment in identity. Nor are we safe from it as we come closer to home, for there it is increasingly in the family, the neighbourhood, indeed in the very spaces where we hoped above all to escape its oppressive and dehumanizing ethos in our search for community outside and beyond institutions. For community itself is in danger of becoming an identity to be managed and secured: a master word, a dead idol to which the living are sacrificed in the logic of its management. The trouble with idols is that they come to replace that to which they should be only pointers, and then instead of taking us beyond ourselves and offering us a future which could be different, they lock us into prescribed and prescriptive identities — ways of being — which block the possibility of transcendence. (Donna Jowett, Rick Harp, Sonja Embree, and Geraldine Finn describe how this works in their respective contributions to this volume.)

Hence our suggestion that community be read as catachresis. Presupposition of its absence or presence constitutes its disavowal as a transcendence which is desired and which cannot be tied down. Transcendence — community — cannot be "managed" and our experience of it is always as of a crisis which breaks through the manageable and familiar, and exposes us as it frees us. Thus, as Karim Benammar says of the "absences of community" in chapter 1, they haunt us, and give us solace but not refuge. One point of our writing then is the interruption of crisis management in the name of "community," in different places, on different levels, but with the same effect of subversion: of putting the received version of "community" into question, disrupting the taken-for-granted knowledges of its realization and value, so that a gap can appear — an absence, an abyss, an aporia— what Geraldine Finn calls a "space-between," where certitudes must be abandoned and creativity and change (i.e. transcendence) are possible.

This collection is not the work of a team but rather an "assemblage" of singularities as described by Barend Kiefte in chapter 9. Far from saying the "same thing," we come from such different places that we cannot even be said to contradict each other when we disagree (in embracing or rejecting deconstruction, for example). What we offer is not a united front, nor even a coalition, but an assemblage of personal histories and poems; cultural analysis, politics and economics; statistics, chemistry and soil science; medieval theology and discussion of the latest horror movies; as well as wide-ranging philosophical commentary. Nevertheless, though we have not made it our goal, nor even the explicit premise of our work, we have each been guided by a sense of reality as differance/difference and blessed by community, different for each of us as transcendence must be, to which we seek to bear common witness in this book.

The Essays

When we began to discuss the possibility of this collection on community, we knew we wanted to combine theory and analysis with something closer to lived experience. As the collection came together, not only did the themes discussed above keep reappearing in a sort of tapestry, but somewhat unexpectedly the essays fell more or less spontaneously into a series of pairs, in which a theoretical discussion of community received a particular specification in one which was more personal and concrete. In chapter 1 for example, "Origins, Occupations, and the Proximity of the Neighbour," Donna Jowett describes her own resistance to those who proclaim allegiance to "community with inclusive or exclusive membership," as she acknowledges participation in the community she has not chosen and which she describes in terms of the "proximity of the neighbour." Not choosing it while being claimed by it constitutes this community as in some sense an "absence" analogous to those described by Benammar in the chapter which follows. With insights developed from the work of Emmanuel Levinas, Jowett makes it clear how the proximity of the neighbour puts one in question, precisely because one is "other," and contests one's occupation of one's place. The response of Jowett and those of her neighbourhood to the predicament of the elderly sisters on her street echoes Benammar's discussion of the "community at the threshold of death," and is the antithesis of the community espoused by social planning or ideology. Indeed, her disclosure of the implicit — and even explicit — tyranny of the wilful creators of "community" in her neighbourhood — the "activists" — reveals a motivation to "community" which undermines itself; which precludes openness to the other, and prevents the possibility of the "solace" that Benammar describes.

In chapter 2, "Absences of Community," Karim Benammar draws on the philosophies of Jean-Luc Nancy, Maurice Blanchot and Alphonso Lingis to describe a "passion for community" which expresses the desire to transcend the everydayness of our individual existence, our existence as individuals, to cross the limits of identity in an exstatic moment. He identifies four situations which can be occasions for this experience of a being-with-others in community outside and beyond already instituted communities: the aesthetic community, the community of lovers, the community at the threshold of death, and the community of those who have nothing in common. They are all moments of open-ended crisis (transcendence), where one loses oneself, forgets who one is, ceases in Kiefte's phrase to be "perceptible and interpretable" (chapter 9), just as one ceases to perceive or interpret the other(s).

Chapter 3, "Native by Nature?" by Rick Harp, speaks from and of the experience of the absence of community among the First Nations people of Canada, and challenges assumptions about Native identity upon which the hypostasis of such communities (by Native and non-Native Canadians alike) depend. Harp's account of "discursive colonialism" makes it clear how little room the oppressor's categories have left for the creation of alternatives to the communities and identities of oppression, to those who originally had no concept of race or of private property in land. How can one envisage a future which is different, he asks, when the identity one is assigned is defined in terms of a mythical past and a tradition constructed to mask the realities of its history? The poignancy of Harp's account is a kind of response to the self-searching of Jowett's meditation on "origins" and "occupation," and a prelude to the "politics of location" discussed by Anna Antonopoulos in relation to 'home.'

Chapter 4, "The Politics of 'Home'" draws on recent material in cultural analysis to disperse the comforting myths about the 'home,' by challenging the opposition of public and private which is their foundation. Antonopoulos discusses how the violence uncovered by the reversal of this binary opposition[4] is (not coincidentally) dramatized in domestic horror movies which have become so popular. Her deconstruction of 'home' reveals the contradictions in its image as at one and the same time the secure foundation for society and the locus of a praxis which is opposed to it. The relationship of women to the home focuses this contradiction in its political and psychic im-plications and effects: women's work as 'home-makers' and mothers in the home is usually invisible (repressed), echoing Freud's account of the *Heim* (home) as *unheimlich* (uncanny) in the same way that his (male) patients found the female genitals uncanny as "the entrance to the former home of all human beings."

Antonopoulos's exposure of the ideological and political con-tradictions of the 'home' and women's relationship to it sets the stage for Sonja Embree's exploration of the psychodynamics of her own feminism in chapter 5, "Mommy Dearest: Women's Studies and the Search for Identity." In this chapter, Embree describes her own strug-gle for a space between the effects of home and the gender identity produced there, and the ideological promises of Women's Studies. The sisterhood and community of the latter claimed her allegiance, but as she discovered "community" cannot be so easily chosen (or prescribed), and acceptance of ideals is not the way to transcendence. The map of Women's Studies, like the categories discussed by Geral-dine Finn in the next chapter, did not seem to apply to the terrain of her own experience. The road she was looking for, beyond the sedi-mented identities of the past and the prescribed identities of her Women's Studies present, was "still feeling its way through," and could not be borrowed from or superimposed by an other. Not even another Mother, like Women's Studies sometimes seems to be.

In chapter 6, "The Space-Between Ethics and Politics. Or More of the Same?," Geraldine Finn returns us to the aporia, the abyss, the absence of community, in the space-between theory and practice, categories and reality, languages and lives, which is the space of Embree's journey. She explains how the categories imposed by the exigencies of politics — the categories of race, gender, sexuality and nation for example, work to reduce us to their own dimensions: to "being-as" a faithful and fulfilling member of a category or class — a good woman, a real Indian, a normal man, for example. And she shows how this categorical imperative of power — to assume an identity — pre-empts the possibility of ethics; of real critique and change which can only come from the excess of being over being-as, the experience of incommensurability between category and reality in the aporia of the "space-between."

Christopher Lind's essay, "When the System Farms the Farmers: What Can We Do About the Saskatchewan Farm Crisis?" poses the question of ethics in the space-between beyond the categories of traditional politics in a more precise, concrete, and focused way — with reference to the current farm crisis in Saskatchewan. His research reveals how the farmers reject the management solutions of "crisis" offered by economic and political experts and call instead for an ethic which expands the ideal of community to include the land itself and a relationship of friendship with it and others. This essay presents yet another perspective on the politics of location and the community we have not chosen, and shows up once again the moral bankruptcy of an economic and epistemological framework which defines "community" prescriptively in terms of discrete identities and "self-interest": mistaking the nature of both the *self* and the *interest* (and the identity) at stake in the crisis of, and the desire for, "community."

In chapter 8, "Poverty," Howard Richards calls for a similar recontextualizing of economics within the framework of ethics and

philosophy in general, and the being-in-relation espoused by John Macmurray and Thomas Aquinas in particular. Richards presents himself, in
the voice and figure of Aquinas, as an opponent of deconstruction and
advocates a return to a metaphysics which encompasses the whole, although the "form" he invites us to strive for and be obedient to (which is
another name for God), does not trap us in either hierarchy or immanence as the deconstructive critique of Western metaphysics has led
us to believe. Far from being a category which contains us, "obedience to
form" on this account is but another way of acknowledging the
transcendence we are seeking in community.

Barend Kiefte's chapter on Gilles Deleuze brings together many
of the themes central to this book in a sustained and systematic
presentation of Deleuze's philosophy — which Kiefte calls an "ontology of difference" — and its implications for ethics and community.
Deleuze's philosophy "can be considered as the dual attempt to think
in terms of events and to make thinking an event" such that the
totalising categories of identity, of being-as upon which fascism
depends, lose their authority as both reality and ideal, in the presence
of "anonymous, pre-individual singularities" and "unlimited becoming" upon which fascism, whether personal or political, has no purchase. Community occurs here as a shifting assemblage — rather like
this book — founded not on similarities of identity or interest narrowly defined, but on the affirmation of difference which is both productive and produced.

Deleuze's epistemology is an ethics because it is an affirmation of
difference and not a retreat from it. The chapter by Eleanor Godway
which follows, "Deconstructing Privilege," could be regarded as an
application of it, as it struggles to renounce the voice and authority of
privileged difference — the privilege of being white — alongside and
in conversation with Audre Lorde and Gayatri Spivak. Deleuze's
ethics is indefinite, like the ethics of the space-between described by
Geraldine Finn. It does not tell us what to do. If it did, if it were
definite, it would cease to be an ethics and become politics, as both

Kiefte and Finn have shown. Audre Lorde makes a similar distinction between poetry and rhetoric. The "passion for community" described by Benammar, the "joyful affirmation" of difference proposed by Barend, the possibilities of "transcendence" in the space-between suggested by Finn, are echoed in the "erotic" of Audre Lorde's poetry and prose. This, we believe, marks the place of community, of the absence of "community," the affirmation of which is at once the premise, the provocation, and the purpose of this book.

Notes

1. *Persons in Relation.* Faber and Faber, London. 1961.
2. Gayatri Spivak, *The Post-Colonial Critic*, Routledge, New York, 1990.
3. Gayatri Spivak, "The Practical Politics of the Open End," *The Post-Colonial Critic*, Routledge, New York, 1990, pp. 95-112.
4. See Godway's development of this theme (from Spivak) in chapter 10 below.

1

Origins, Occupation, and the Proximity of the Neighbour[1]

Donna Jowett

There is a normative discourse of "community" which aspires to it as a good, and which makes very many arresting claims concerning the value of community and the tragedy of its demise or disintegration in North America and Western Europe. It is not clear whether communities in other places are thought to be thriving or also suffering, but there is a tendency to assume that "we"[2] are the ones with the interesting problem of endangering "our own" communities through the very values and structures which are characteristic of "our" society. Speakers positioned within this discourse may be bureaucrats or radicals or both together since "our" society offers reasonably lucrative employment to people prepared to be both. This discourse permits a certain amount of critical commentary about society in general, but does not think to ask any questions about the ideal of community itself, or even about any actual community. Since "community" is endangered it must therefore be saved or rescued or re-membered — through community development, community centres, community liaison "officers," whole departments and ministries of community services, through the ever proliferating number of sites where community is "worked for" — but not questioned. The discourse of community is respectable and respects itself; it commands allegiance to its organizing concept even if or especially when a speaker positioned within this discourse speaks mainly about the loss or disintegration of community.

This discourse is ripe for critical analysis, but that analysis would, perhaps, most appropriately come from someone who can use the word "community" with some knowledge of it.[3] This means that I will not be able to offer such an analysis here, for I do not have this knowledge of community that would permit me to "save" it or defend it from the discourse which presently surrounds it. It may be that this should not constitute much of a problem; how could I begin to seek the meaning of something beyond its discursive formulation and circulation? But I have found that I am arrested at the level of my own condition of not knowing anything about community, and rather than track the discourse of it in order to arrive at a positivity consisting of some certainty or knowledge of how the discourse works and what its effects clearly are, I need to stay with my ignorance a while longer. It may be the case that there are certain factors responsible for this state of ignorance which tracking the discourse of community would permit me to overlook or cover over. Thinking about community has had the effect of putting my origins and occupation of space into question and the question of origins and occupation of space must be considered also in connection to the possible goodness of community.

* * *

In my neighbourhood, in my teaching at university and amongst my friends, I do not know of anyone else who was, as I was, born here. It is clear that many such other people exist, I just do not happen to know any of them personally. And this city, unlike the iconized cities of New York, London and Paris, does not command much loyalty — being born here does not confer any enviable status, and to be born here and still be living here decades later elicits expressions of condolence, bewilderment or polite silence. Nevertheless, my work, social relations and political sentiments bring me frequently into contact with people who talk about community, about "their" communities, about the need for community, about community development, about community care, community activism and so on. They seem to know what community is or needs to be, and I, perhaps because I have lived here virtually all my life, do not. I am a stranger amongst these speakers of community, having neither the strangeness of this place nor its deep hold on me in common with anyone I happen to know. I do not consciously speak on behalf of, or deliberately represent any community, and no one demands this of me since as a white, English speaking Canadian no one requires me to re-present anything in particular. My lifelong bonds of attachment to and continuity with a particular environment, geography, climate, architecture, all of which reverberate with associations from childhood to present day, set me apart from those who inhabit the communities on offer to me. Changes, absences and losses are inscribed within my daily habitat, making them easier to bear because I regularly have the occasion to mark them and to mourn them in a way that affirms the value of those things I have loved without having control over. My life is in-dis-sociable from the place where I have lived it and this has seemingly created a strange confusion or blankness in my mind regarding the question of community.

I am aware that mine is a rare case, an exception within the milieu I inhabit, which includes academics, other "professionals," students, and development and social workers, none of whom were born here and many of whom have immigrated from other countries. I do not share the experience they have in common of being strangers, immigrants, of being torn between their homeplaces, or first languages and this place, this language, of belonging to more than one place and to no particular place. Both within and without the mores of my own place, language, class, culture and time, there is something anomalous or perhaps anachronistic about my experience.

I am confused about the meaning of community, having never had the experience of choosing to belong or being forced to leave one. I feel naive in these matters, thinking that community is something about which you have no choice. You are born in a certain place, amongst certain people and for better or for worse this setting and these relations are the givenness of your community. You cannot choose it, although you may, depending on your wealth, privilege, nationality, freely decide to leave it, or you may be forced to leave it through political and economic hardship, terrorism and/or the effects of colonization and post-colonial diaspora. Whether you immigrate as a privileged investor/professional or a political refugee, you will most likely make an effort to locate or even live amongst people like yourself, other strangers in a new place, but similar to the people you left behind. This effort is an aspect of the givenness of community — what pulls you back to "your community" is an absence of choice about where you were born, what language you were born into, what relations, expressions and values you inherited. Dislocated, disconnected and alienated from the taken-for-grantedness of this familiar absence of choice, you seek it out again, yearning, perhaps, for what is reassuring about it — you do not have to choose it, you are not free to choose it, you are not free not to choose it. This in no way means you are not capable of criticizing it. It may mean this is the only thing you have to criticize. It may mean that this is one of the things you have to love the most. The new circumstances of your life, or perhaps the very circumstances that drove you to leave your former life may also provide a critical distance and perspective from the values and customs of your community of origin. Of course you do not have to leave your community in order to be critical of it or to love it — there is no necessary critical or loving perspective to be derived from either staying or going. Those who advocate either travel or work in "other cultures" as a way of gaining a critical perspective on their own should remember that "adventure," colonization and the neo-colonial, on-going quest for new markets has not historically resulted in the adventurous ones gaining much critical perspective on their culture of origin.

Sometimes, when I do not disguise my confusion about the question of community, I am told I am thinking of it in the wrong way. The speakers of community are not talking about the incidental and contingent accident of birth, but about *political* communities based on shared, even passionate commitments to issues of social justice. This has a compelling sound to it — I feel as if I should indicate that I know what is being talked about here — but in truth, my confusion is not lessened. These incidental and accidental features of birth, country, language, and culture of origin do not appear less important than the issue of the particular political convictions espoused by the speaker. A white, English speaker, speaking here, in the city of my birth, may take these features for granted, having the privilege of being blind to their significance. But whether these features are taken for granted, challenged as expressions of political privilege, or actively sought as the basis for "strengthening communities," there is little indication that language, culture, nationality have ceased to inform the idea of community. The only people who appear anxious to disown or deny this are white and tend to think of themselves as politically progressive, or liberal; they speak about community building, community choices, about choosing to work for meaningful communities. While I do not think that acknowledging the significance of one's origins necessarily translates into either a right wing or left wing political outlook, I am inclined to think that the denial of it stems from a particular form of unearned and unexamined privilege and that the continued practice of this denial perpetuates that privilege rather than exposing it or facilitating its demise.

What is interesting to me is that the white liberals and "progressives" who speak most about community are often very anxious to prove that there are no constraining or exclusionary elements at work in their "choice" of community. But then what is the meaning of community I wonder if it is open to all travellers, if it is more along the lines of a bus depot, where everyone freely comes and goes, with no one staying very long, with "difference" and "otherness" available for our interested albeit detached observation, but not interfering with our agenda or travel plans? Unchosen affiliations and attachments seem to have no place in the open political communities those who speak to me, in my ignorance about community, tell me about. What they tell me is that it does not matter where you come from, what counts is what you believe in, what you are struggling for, and how hard you are prepared to work to create meaningful communities.

This paradigmatically white, middle-class and politically correct view of community is contested on just about every other front and from quite disparate political positions. It is contested by white supremacists who advance a closed, blood-based, identarian notion of community and origins. It is contested by Québec nationalists who know that without linguistic and cultural protection, they will soon find themselves belonging to those amorphous communities which claim that "where you come from" does not matter, but where only English is spoken. And it is contested by people and groups referred to by the Canadian state as "visible minorities" — immigrants and aboriginal peoples. Such groups do not have the privilege of denying that "where they come from" is of no consequence. The paradigmatically white and well-intentioned denial of this strikes me as equally if not more outrageous than overt expressions of racism, white supremacy, Anglo chauvinism or anti-semitism.

· Where I come from matters to me and I didn't choose it and it is not always a source of strength or pleasure and it confers unearned privilege on me and there is no way of discounting it except through acts of hypocrisy and bad faith. But there is no moral leverage, no high ground to be gained from acknowledging this. It is a contingent and essential "given" which is the occasion for both ethics and the refusal of ethics. My absence of choice about it is the situation in which the possibility of ethics arises.[4] This possibility is foreclosed, dismissed, displaced or transferred onto a concept/metaphor about communities of choice in which my attachment to place and time would cease to be contested because they would be denied, in which they would not have the occasion to be revealed as operative and without entitlement or justice. In owning up to my attachments I may begin to glimpse the sort of investment I have in them. I may also then be obliged to notice that this investment is not founded in any sort of *a priori* entitlement, that my being-here and what it means to me, even its preciousness, has contingency and not rights or justice at its base.

But I am still thinking about the struggle to create meaningful communities. I suppose that means communities you choose and go on choosing because you are enriched and fulfilled by them — they give you something and it is something you want. If they gave you what you did not want then you would probably opt out of them and look or work for some sort of other community that was more to your liking. This makes a certain amount of sense, but then I find myself wondering if there is any difference between communities of self-interest — the ones where you find what you want and are filled up and enriched and expanded by them — and Club Med vacations or health spas or golf clubs.

My interlocutors sometimes grow exasperated with me. They ask me if I don't have a need for a socially affirming connection with a group, a connection that would permit me to transcend my individuality, and through which I would realize an ec-static communion with something larger than myself. This is a stunning sort of question. I am stunned by the instrumentality it takes for granted; the sanctioned "choice" or use of a group to provide me with some benefit or alteration in my consciousness. This effect, the question also assumes, would not come through one's everyday relations with people, with friends; it must be deliberately sought and constituted as a group experience organized to achieve certain ends. Perhaps the question offers a commentary on the paucity of "everyday relations," a sad resignation to fragmentation and atomization. But in its quest for transcendence it assumes and invokes a blind instrumentalism which will never produce the ends of either social affirmation or transcendence for which it aims. It hungers for what it has in fact given up on. Its devouring appetite requires the construction and consumption of prefabricated group experiences, easily named, not too difficult to join, scheduled according to one's "leisure" or vacation time.

Ec-static communion: the term itself is a fertile oxymoron: to be outside of one-self and at *one-with*. This greater unity involves the forfeit of the self; the self is not made larger in this, but is left behind. Or is it? If, in ec-static movement, the oneself is given up, forfeited, then there would be nothing remaining to be taken up into communion; perhaps it is not that the self is forfeited, but that it is held hostage by what it cannot command or control.[5] Ec-static communion is a hot, breathless point of arrest, impossible to choose or will or dominate. And it comes with no guarantees. This does not mean that I am against it or that I have never experienced it. When it has come to me it has not been through my efforts but as a gift I am both grateful for and ambivalent about. In my own case this excessive gift has been associated with love and with death and the relations involved here, their power and force, have had little to do with my choices except in so far as I have wanted to be open to what I had no choice about experiencing. What is larger than me also resists me, there is no way of incorporating it into myself except at its expense. It claims me; it is not mine to claim. The point is precisely *not* to expand myself through incorporating it; if I do this I will not be visited again by its claim. I will have lost it by consuming it.[6]

Perhaps this is the loss of community which some speak about, communities of consumption, consuming communities, communities consumed and therefore lost and absent. Having lived in the same place so long I do not feel I have any consumer choice when it comes to the question of community. The on-going fiction or appeal of "community" in politically correct, white circles is that it is ours to choose but the "it" of it is already assumed as existing and as good. And who will say that these communities of choice are chosen for their resonance with communities we had no freedom in choosing?

* * *

Certainly, one of the key questions concerning community must be about its assumed goodness. It is assumed by most speakers of community that community is good. Clearly, they think it is good for the people in it, but then what of the people not in it? Perhaps they will not care, having communities of their own with different values, practices and idioms which are good for them. Or perhaps those not in a particular community are harmed by their exclusion and have no ready made communities waiting in the wings to be chosen by them. Perhaps they are systematically excluded from the communities available for consumption. This is not so benign a thing at all, but then neither is the fanatical relativism of the market place approach to communities which turns us all into consumers of fashionable or in-group orthodoxies. Perhaps community should not be approached as necessarily and only a good thing even for those who are "in" community. Perhaps what is or could be good about community, good in a way that is not just about me getting what I want out of one, requires that we not even assume community, never mind its goodness. Perhaps, if there is such a possibility as a "good community" it will have more to do with its claim on me than mine on it. But I have got way ahead of myself here, because I still do not know what community means. Apparently composed of others, these others have so far been faceless, silent, erased in the anonymous totality invoked by the word "community." I cannot begin with community; since I have no handy knowledge of community, it could only appear in these lines as an abstraction or projection of my own wish for a welcoming space. This wish is not meaningless or insignificant, but the goodness of community, if such a thing is possible, lies elsewhere.

* * *

A guiltless responsibility, whereby I am none the less open to an accusation of which no alibi, spatial or temporal could clear me. It is as if the other established a relationship or a relationship were established whose whole intensity consists in not presupposing the idea of community. A responsibility stemming from a time before my freedom ... Responsibility for my neighbour, for the stranger or sojourner, to which nothing in the rigorously ontological order binds me — nothing in the order of the thing, of the something, of number or causality.[7]

According to Levinas, "responsibility for my neighbour" — who may be and remain a stranger or sojourner — is not a matter of choice; it is given through proximity alone, beyond or outside of any contract or agreement into which I might enter. This proximity makes me subject to the neighbour whose existence is a feature of my own — who subjects me perhaps to the smell of food cooking, to loud music, to a dandelion-filled lawn, to fencing or the absence of fencing, to the material substance and ephemera of her daily existence. My own space and my habitation of it are no longer purely my own (there was never such a time, except in the mind of liberal social-contract theorists); "my" space and even my being are contested by the proximity of the neighbour who riles me to defend "my place in the sun." (Does the addition planned for her house diminish the amount of sunlight I will receive through the windows of my own?) My sense of entitlement to this place and to the extension of my being in and through this place is aroused, but it is aroused only because it has been put into question. In response I can assert a "right" to my place in the sun — and in fact this is the way things most often proceed, at least in this neighbourhood, in this city. But, as Levinas points outs in his epigrammatic preface to *Otherwise than Being,* the sense of entitlement expressed in the statement, "that is my place in the sun" is how the whole usurpation of the world begins, begins again, is renewed and replenished. My occupation of space, an unavoidable occupation of space that is justified by no entitlement outside the arbitrariness of the law, is what the proximity of the neighbour contests.

This neighbour no-wise constitutes the beginnings of a self-willed and consciously chosen community. We may or may not speak the same language, share similar beliefs, have anything at all in common. It is not because the neighbour is either similar to or different from me that I am subject to her; and, in any case, she is both of these together, similar because different, or as Gayatri Chakravorty Spivak puts it: "People are similar not by virtue of being similar, but by virtue of producing a differential, or by virtue of thinking of themselves as other than a self-identical example of the species."[8] It is not because I put the community first, consigning her to a functional role, a function of the organizing concept of community and then agree, through its totalizing mediation, to recognize her, to behave benevolently towards her. It is proximity and not community which produces the relation with the neighbour I have not chosen. What I then choose in the face of this is a matter of ethics, of responsibility. If I regard my occupation of space, my being and pleasure in being as a matter of entitlement I may, through altruism, be moved to behave benevolently or charitably, but this comes from my sense of fortification and authority; it does not put that fortification and authority into question, it enables me to go on believing in them, to go on producing them. I may be prepared to give up some surplus, something I have no need for, to her, to others, to "charities." But I do not give up my life, my persistence in being, my occupation of this and other spaces. It is not that self-effacement to the point of non-existence is required here; I would follow this course only if I were more concerned to be judged a saint (to be judged "right") than to learn how to live with the neighbour. Perhaps this is why Levinas acknowledges that there is nothing more burdensome than a neighbour.

There is a dilemma here. I cannot claim entitlement to this place, to the accident of being born here. I do not feel I have any particular "right" to it although this in no way diminishes its hold on me. I have no entitlement, no more right to this patch of sunlight than anyone else, but I nevertheless occupy it. I cannot not occupy it, whether it is a here or an elsewhere. I occupy a place which is not mine through any right or entitlement; it is simply that I am here, having no choice about being somewhere. But when my neighbour disturbs my naive perseverance in being, which she may do by being welcoming or persecuting, I must justify myself before her. If she is welcoming then I am indebted already to her and through attempting to establish friendly and reciprocal relations I will try to erase my debt, get us on an "equal footing" so that I will no longer recognize any debt to her to which I did not contract. I will then be free to relate to her as if I had chosen her, covering over the fact that I was designated by her before recognizing her. If she is persecuting or bothersome I may stake my claim to my territory more firmly, in no way open to admitting that my being here is without rights or entitlement, and hence that I am indebted already to her, "open to an accusation of which no alibi, spatial or temporal, could clear me." A "guiltless responsibility" is produced by her proximity, her welcome or rebuff or need, the responsibility to justify my place in the sun for which no possible justification exists. This is why I am subject to and a hostage of this neighbour who summons me through proximity to acknowledge the multiple conundrum of response-ability uttered in the words, "here I am."[9]

Neighbours need not be persecuting in order for me to stand accused, to exist in the accusative case in relation to them. It is not my "I" that determines proximity but proximity which determines "me." I come into being through proximity, proximity produces me as a subject, an "I" who comes after the others and through the others — mothers, fathers, relatives, neighbours, teachers, strangers, friends, all those on whom my life depends. Because of them there is a me who occupies a place, who occupies without justice, this place and not some other. What could justice mean here but a justification, a social-contract, a commensurability between what sustains my life and what I am able to pay back? But there can be no such commensurability, this would be an injustice.[10] It is not only that I do not have the capacity to balance the scales, there are no scales of equivalence here that can trade off so many breaths against so many others. Justice, regarded as a weighing or settling of accounts which would then absolve me of my condition of indebtedness, is not just. The only ap-proximation of justice possible is a recognition that there is no justice in me being here. And so my answer is also my confession, "here I am" — accused and answerable to my neighbour. Whether or not she is of "my community," she is the only community there can be. And similar to the community from which I came, I have no choice about her, but different from my unreflective attitude towards the community from which I came, I cannot presuppose anything about her, any commonality stemming from language, belief or culture. But even if this commonality exists, I cannot use it as a way of determining my relations with her unless I am content with xenophobia as my ethical code. I cannot presuppose commonality because, as Spivak points out, we are similar by virtue of producing a differential, which means that I cannot presuppose commonality, or I cannot presuppose it very far, even when my neighbour speaks the same language, was born in the same place, shares my beliefs. According to Levinas, "It is not because the neighbour would be recognized as belonging to the same genus as me that he concerns me. He is precisely *other*. The community with him begins in my obligation to him."[11] Proximity to a neighbour throws me into unflattering relief.

Proximity is not gratitude or benevolence; it is the unchosen, unchooseable situation bearing down on me, exposing me and summoning me to give an account which puts my own occupation of place at risk. This risk is a possibility for community, for a meaning of community which neither divests itself of its attachment to origins nor claims any naturalized or moral right to them. But I do not arrive at this risk by presupposing the idea of the community; if there is community it is produced through the relations I maintain in proximity and not through programmes of self-improvement or group consumption.

But how can what is good, or what I am beginning to think of as potentially good, take root in what is not chosen, in the situation of proximity to a neighbour?

Nothing determines or requires this goodness. Unchosen proximity is also a situation of potential conflict, potential harm. Proximity presents me with what I did not ask for or summon before me. It is a given of existence in the world, but apparently such a strange and problematic given that recourse has been sought to separation, enclosure, to the many forms of apartheid intended to control or control for proximity through the specification and regulation of communities of the Same. This sameness is actually never successfully totalizing; these communities and regimes are never vigilant enough to completely succeed in guarding against "impurity." The Same exists only by displacing the difference within it to "others" marked as inferior through the burden of difference they are forced to carry so that the Same can continue to hallucinate its sameness, purity and privilege to itself. The uncertainties and risks of proximity become the certain brutality of enforced separation, separation that can only exist through brutality and hypervigilance, through the still and powerfully operative idea that certain others should go back to where they came from and if this is not possible stay in cordoned off areas of social and imaginative life so that which regards itself as the Same will not be contested.

The possible goodness of proximity is that it invites or summons me to account for my occupation of space; it exposes me, even in what I may love most, to scrutiny and questioning. Freedom and entitlement may matter more to me than running this risk; they often do. I can turn away from the claim of the neighbour, but although what I call freedom permits this, there are no "good" words or even neutral words to describe rejection, refusal or persecution of the neighbour.[12] Language, freedom and the law permit me to "justify" my turning away; I can and do "justify" my about face from the claim of the neighbour upon me, but this justification is the beginning of injustice; I am given over to the pursuit of injustice in my justification for my occupation of place for which no justification exists. Unless recourse is made to a history of injustice which brought people like me to this place and usurped it from those here before me. Or unless the accident and unchosenness in my being here before anyone else, my first occupation, were regarded as entitlement to refuse the entry and occupation of others.

Where or what is the justice of *occupation,* of occupied territories? An odd word, "occupation," used in the political vocabulary of this century to mean unjustly being in a place that does not "belong" to you, where you maintain your presence only through the exertion or threat of force. My own occupation of space is a restriction of that space as well as a utilization of it. If, in attempting to justify it, I make claims on it because I occupy it, then justice means no more than occupation. There is a certain logic to this, but when in proximity my occupation is exposed as without entitlement, the injustice of occupation becomes apparent. This is not merely an inconsistency; it is not a contradiction. It reveals the ethical dilemma at the heart of our occupation of space: that it is not ethical and that ethics begins with the blow or impact of this situation already upon me, too late for me to excuse or back my way out of, the whole intensity of which consists in "not presupposing the idea of community" through which I could rationalize my being here. I can not subordinate my neighbour to a reflection, representation or functional cog of a community as some way of knowing whether or not I owe her anything. "Presupposing the idea of community" renders the question of the neighbour into one of either belonging or not belonging, being inside or outside; it subordinates the exigent ethical relationship with the neighbour to various terms, concepts, and ideals in which we hope to find ourselves. Actually, I *can* subordinate my neighbour to my idea of community; in fact, I am encouraged to do this through the discourse of community, but this is not justice or ethics or even the beginning of community but only an expression of functional, totalizing, identarian thinking, which, if it is not accompanied or followed by a massive and picayune system of jurisprudence, would soon reveal the logic of the Inquisition at its core.

* * *

A short time ago, a "community activist" from my neighbourhood was interviewed on the radio. She suggested that one way of practising "respect for the environment" while fostering "community responsibility" would be to form a committee or group to inspect neighbourhood garbage. This group would regularly patrol backyards and garbage pails, making sure that everyone is recycling and composting. Committing a garbage crime, e.g., throwing out too much garbage, or the wrong garbage, or not composting, etc., would result in some sort of censure or possibly even a fine being levied by the garbage surveillance unit. The speaker thought that the risk of social ostracism or censure would do a lot to promote "environmentalism" while at the same time it would strengthen "community ties." This strong and self-regulating community would be based on garbage correctness and not skin colour or language or age or sex, although class remains as an unspoken basis of environmental correctness, for it is home-owners with backyards and recycling boxes and more than one garbage receptacle who can be most virtuous in the treatment of their waste. The self-constitution of this community obeys the same principles of exclusion and inclusion of more familiarly constituted communities, but it is clearly apparent here that exclusion is a punishment for a moral/political failure, which the virtuous home-owner, with political and legal rights to occupation of this particular space, would be concerned to avoid. In a way it is refreshing to hear someone speak so openly about the surveillance, regulation and censure informing their idea of community, but it is, at the same time, chilling to have it spoken in the name of what passes for "progressive" or radical politics.

* * *

I have something else in mind, something closer, something that is not yet community, yet it is not so far from it as the community garbage surveillance unit. There are two women, sisters in their nineties, who live across the street from me. We rarely speak, but we often wave to each other and I, along with other neighbours, shovel their laneway in the winter time. This is not much. I often see them struggling to the store a few blocks away, always one or the other, never both together. From what I observe, they own only one pair of boots between them, and these are worn until June of each year and then reappear again in September. They are very frail and also shy, shy perhaps because they are frail. My Christmas gesture of a fruit basket is hardly adequate to their needs. Still, I along with others in the neighbourhood watch them carefully; it is not my eyes alone that regard them as they sun themselves on July afternoons, sitting on their ancient lawn chairs, backs turned to the sun, heads nodding on necks that wobble like wounded birds. They are so old, so delicate, so without means, and yet they enjoy the sun and tend their small unruly flower garden. I watch them carefully, wondering at the mystery of their daily routines: the small containers of water thrown over the railing of their front porch morning and evening; their alternating, never joint scrutiny of the hollyhocks that grow tall outside their front window; the habit of one who comes outside to comb and dry her sparse and fine white hair in the summer, her hand trembling as she pulls the comb through the wet strands. They ask for nothing, but their vulnerability and need accuse all of us who regard them, we who are farther away from death than they are. This is an inescapable accusation for which there is no adequate response; no amount of charity will prolong their lives, the lives they show they cherish, as I cherish mine, helplessly. The accusation born out of what both separates and connects us is more near and more devastating than justice or "the community"; it is given through proximity not of my choosing. If there is the possibility for goodness here — which would still not be justice, cannot be justice — it is because of the haunting and relentless claim of my neighbours on my life, my place in the sun, my occupation of space.

* * *

Consciousness responds to a situation that is already upon it, before choice, freedom or intentionality; "good intentions" come after the fact and so "consciousness is always late for the rendez-vous with the neighbour,"[13] an assignation summoning me to justify myself where I am exposed as without justification. There is no organization of sameness or difference to cure this, no community which by its welcome absolves me from my lateness or constitutes the neighbour and the relations I maintain with her as a product of my choice, freedom, will. Or, rather, there are communities which aim to do this; this seems to be the currency of community today, in the circles with which I am familiar, the circles of community seekers and makers, whose deployment of the concept, full of zealotry and good intentions, is the erasure not only of the risk of community, but the risk of its goodness.

Notes

1. "The proximity of" and "rendezvous with the neighbour" are key terms for Emmanuel Levinas. See especially, *Otherwise Than Being or Beyond Essence.* trans. Alphonso Lingis (The Hague: Martinus Nijhoff Publishers, 1981). I address these terms more directly in the second part of this essay.
2. I use quotation marks around "we" and "our" in this context not only in order to indicate that it is not very clear who or what is included within these words, but also to emphasize their possessiveness. This possessiveness is one starting point for reflection upon the meaning of community.
3. Iris Marion Young in "The Ideal of Community and the Politics of Difference," in *Feminism/Postmodernism.* Ed. Linda J. Nicholson. (New York: Routledge, 1990) pp. 300-323, criticizes the ideal of community, relying on readings of Adorno and Derrida to question the homogeneity, the privileging of sameness and identity which characterize such thinkers as Michael Sandel and Carol Gilligan, whom Young identifies as communitarian or identarian. Although Young is also critical of individualism and sceptical about the discourse of rights, her critical engage-

ment with the ideal of community devolves into praise for the powerful attrac-
tions of large urban centres, their cultural diversity, multiplicity of activities, art
galleries, glittering lights and ethnic restaurants, all offering possible encounters with "difference." She writes that "instead of the ideal of community,
we begin with our positive experience of city life to form a vision of the good
society." This scandalously one-sided view of the "good life" afforded by the
cities she names, New York, Boston and San Francisco, is such a serious problem
in this essay that it is not likely to be corrected by tinkering with a passage or
concept here and there. I would say, however, that one of the reasons Young's
critique of the ideal of community ends up where it does is that she doesn't *stay*
with the question of community; she doesn't take it seriously enough; she wants
to move on to an alternative "vision," which amounts to nothing more than
praise for the inexhaustibility of consumerism and an alibi — albeit not a strong
one — for staying with the question of community. The fact that she identifies
her approach as "deconstructive" is part of another problem — not the problem
of deconstruction, but the problem of what is done in its name, which may
return after all to be part of a problem *for* deconstruction.

4. "To be without a choice can seem to be violence only to an abusive or hasty and
    imprudent reflection, for it precedes the freedom non-freedom couple, but
    thereby sets up a vocation that goes beyond the limited and egoistic fate of him
    who is only for-himself, and washes his hands of the faults and misfortunes that
    do not begin in his own freedom or in his present." Levinas, *Otherwise than
    Being*, p. 116.

5. "The self is through and through a hostage, older than the ego, prior to prin-
    ciples... It is through the condition of being hostage that there can be in the
    world pity, compassion, pardon and proximity — even the little there is, even
    the simple, 'After you, sir.'" Emmanuel Levinas, *Otherwise than Being*, p. 117.

6. Trinh T. Minh-ha in *Woman, Native, Other: Writing Postcoloniality and Feminism.*
    (Bloomington: Indiana University Press, 1989) criticizes the consuming attitude,
    the attitude of consumption which colonizing groups bring to their encounters
    with "difference." I would say that whether or not the demand is for an "authen-
    tic difference" or for my double, my perfect likeness, I am hoping to expand
    myself through its consumption. If I have the power to demand it, to demand
    that it make itself present to me in the name of either sameness or difference as a
    condition of acknowledging its presence at all, then we have passed beyond
    food metaphors of incorporation and consumption and into socially and
    economically informed consumerism. Nothing within the logic of consumerism
    exists for itself, it exists so that I may own it, benefit from it, or increase my
    knowledge. This logic not only drives the economy, but distorts souls. I can feel
    good about myself when I am a spectator at the performance of someone else's
    culture or community; I think paying money to see "exhibits" in museums or
    "ethnic dancing" in other similar corralled areas qualifies me as someone who is
    open to and respects other cultures. When I shop for a community of my own I
    am hoping for satisfaction, for commensurability between what I want and what

I find. To paraphrase Trinh: what I value and look for is, fortunately, what I only always/never find.

7.   Emmanuel Levinas, "Ethics as first philosophy," in *The Levinas Reader*. Ed. Sean Hand. (Oxford: Basil Blackwell, 1989), pp. 83-84.

8.   Spivak goes on to say, "It seems to me that the emancipatory project is more likely to succeed if one thinks of other people as being different; ultimately, perhaps absolutely different. On a very trivial level, people are different from the object of emancipatory benevolence." Gayatri Chakravorty Spivak, *The Post-Colonial Critic: Interviews, Strategies, Dialogues* (New York: Routledge, 1990), p. 136.

9.   Levinas makes frequent use of the response-ability of the answer "here I am" throughout his work. See, for only one example, "Substitution," in *The Levinas Reader*, p. 104: "The word *I* means *here I am*, answering for everything and for everyone. Responsibility for the others has not been a return to oneself, but an exasperated contracting, which the limits of identity cannot retain."

10.   Derrida in "Force of Law: 'The Mystical Foundation of Authority'," trans. Mary Quaintance, *Cardozo Law Review*, 11 (1990): 919-1078, distinguishes justice from the law. The law approaches justice as a system of weights, balances, equivalences and commensurability. What is called justice is the law, and to the extent that justice is understood and practised as equity, it is unjust with respect to what is incommensurable. The law in its ordering, reducing, synthesizing and blindness does not have time for justice. "Justice in itself, if such a thing exists" is outside or beyond the law. "Deconstruction is justice" because it refuses the injustice of commensurability.

11.   Levinas, *Otherwise than Being*, p. 87.

12.   Levinas, *Otherwise than Being*, p. 6: "The impossibility of declining responsibility is reflected only in the scruple or remorse which precedes or follows this refusal."

13.   Levinas, *Collected Philosophical Papers*. trans. Alphonso Lingis (The Hague: Martinus Nijhoff Publishers, 1987), p. 97.

2

Absences of Community[1]

Karim Benammar

> *Il n'est loisible à quiconque de ne pas appartenir à mon absence*
> *de communauté — (No-one is at leisure not to belong to my*
> *absence of community.)*
>
> Georges Bataille[2]

The passion for community is the passion of our ex-static selves to transcend individuality and to project ourselves as members of a group, community, or society. But this project is doomed if we proclaim our allegiance to a community on the basis of common needs or common goals, common attributes, skills or defects. The passion for community is not realized in the social organization of a group or club with inclusive or exclusive membership. Our passion for community delineates *absences* of community. In these empty, desolate spaces to which we are drawn, the singular self abandons its striving for immanence, without quite forging ties of belonging, brotherhood, community. As Jean-Luc Nancy noted, community is a search for *communion* with the divine. For him, this is a search without issue in which we are all engaged. And, as he also claims, community is not something that has been lost, but it is something yet to come.[3]

It is the "insistent and still unheard demand for community"[4] which gives rise to *absences* of community, ephemeral or virtual communities of those who have no community.[5] The absences of community are explored here in four places by briefly illuminating the traces they leave in our midst: traces of the aesthetic community, the community of lovers, the community on the threshold of death, and the community of those who have nothing in common. We must think of these ephemeral communities as *absences of community* to which we are forced to belong, to which we are not at leisure not to belong. These absences of community haunt and give solace, but not refuge, to our ecstatic individuality.

The Passion For Community

The desire for community haunts our contemporary societies, which are splintered into a myriad of individual rights and positions, fragmented into incommensurable and incommunicable claims, aspirations and satisfactions. For Jean-Paul Sartre, communism, with its promise of a world open to the values and humanity of all through shared effort and labour, was "the unsurpassable horizon of our time."[6] Communism represented, for a whole generation of French intellectuals,[7] a search for the ideology of community and solidarity, while the heedless obsession of capitalism relegated freedom, happiness, and discourse to the private sphere, making them the prerogative and responsibility of individual affirmation. And yet, long before the political demise of communism and the victory by default of capitalist ideology, it had been recognized that the passion for community can be satisfied neither by what its members have "in common"[8] nor by their "equally satisfied needs"[9]: the exigency of community projects itself far beyond the communist ideal, beyond political organization, beyond ideology.

The passion for community haunts not only society, but also the individual in her ecstatic longing, her search for finitude. The individual self cannot find the ground and completion of its own actions, experiences, fantasies or desires within itself; it projects itself outside of itself, ex-statically.[10] This ex-static longing is defined only as the impossibility of absolute immanence or self-fulfilled individuality. The singular self does not find its being within itself; incomplete, it does not desire recognition but contest,[11] seeking the other through ecstatic and often violent desire.

This ecstatic search for the other is the passion for community. For Yukio Mishima, the group, through its shared suffering and openness to death, signified ex-static transgression of individuality and represented the possibility of a new level of experience and existence:

> Only through the group, I realized — through sharing the suffering of the group — could the body reach that height of existence that the individual alone could never attain. And for the body to reach that level at which the divine might be glimpsed, a dissolution of the individuality was necessary. The tragic quality of the group was also necessary — the quality that constantly raised the group out of the abandon and torpor into which it was prone to lapse, leading it on to ever-mounting shared suffering, and so to death, which was the ultimate suffering. The group must be open to death — which meant of course, that it must be a community of warriors ...[12]

The group here represents the mechanism for attaining that which lies beyond the group, in the dissolution of death which tears apart the individual as well as the community. And yet Mishima's community too is ephemeral, an ecstatic passion for an idealized community of warriors, bound by the intangible, and bound for nothingness.

The passion for community manifests itself in three ways: first, a political desire for solidarity, reflected in the false communities of groups, teams, unions, or nations. Second, the individual longing of the self to escape from its own immanence, to ex-statically transcend itself by seeking the other. Third (and this notion is more abstract than the first two), the desire to transcend oneself towards death, to belong to a community defined by the impending dissolution of the individual.

But the passion for community goes beyond the longing for a social order such as promised by communism, beyond the shared experiences of the group, and beyond what any of us have in common with each other. Both Jean-Luc Nancy and Maurice Blanchot have sought to rethink the notion of community on a different basis, taking up the challenge in the writings and passion of Georges Bataille, who understood the infinite and endless ecstatic passion of the individual. For us, the question has become even more acute: what possibility of community is there for a postmodern, fragmented self?

In his essay *The Inoperative Community*, Nancy asks what remains of our notion of community: almost nothing, it seems. Its myths have been suspended, its philosophy exhausted, its politics have been judged by history. Despite this bleak assessment, Nancy claims there is both a resistance of and an insistence on community. This community does not lie in our past, the idea of a "lost community" is a fantasy. Instead, the community lies ahead of us: it is still to be discovered. And it is not the exigency of a common work or labour, but what escapes the work by leaving us exposed to one another.[13]

Nancy's major insight is that the community cannot be tied to work or production, but is *unworking*.[14] The unworking community does not realize itself through the production and work of its members, through co-operatively erected skyscrapers or stock exchanges, through the wars and famines of our "community of nations," or through political constitutions and philosophies of Reason in History. Instead, the passion for an unworking community is a search for communion with the *sacred* in Bataille's sense: "What I had earlier called the sacred, a name that is perhaps purely pedantic ... is fundamentally nothing other than the unleashing of passions."[15] This notion of the sacred is perhaps not unlike the notion of divine which Mishima sought to glimpse through the dissolution of individuality and exposure to death.

The Aesthetic Community

The dispossession of the autonomous self through its ecstatic desire for communication is constitutive of human reality; it is this experience that determines our singularity, the passion of our being.[16] For Blanchot, there is the ephemeral community of writers, who compose for those they do not and will never know, the anonymous body of readers and writers on the other side of words. We write at anonymous distance for unknown friends, others not engaged in a project with us, others who do not work for or with us, others who have nothing in common with us.

What matters is not that we have in common the toil and euphoria of writing. Our evanescent thoughts and efforts do not constitute a literary production or body of texts, but our anonymous communication delineates ties of friendship and the ghostly shape of our humanity. Writing, communicating, is displacing oneself, it is engaging one's being beyond oneself, beyond the limits of the self; we are never freed from this ecstatic desire. And yet we are never able to write transparently, to completely transcend our immanence by pouring all of ourselves into the writing, without restraint. We are unable to write with translucent honesty, incapable of recording the diary of our singular self for which our dearest friend would have to renounce us. Our passion for communication, at its limit, is again without issue.

Blanchot only proposes this negative community, in which the aesthetic articulation of writing signifies as a doomed effort at ecstatic communication, but which nevertheless points to a ghostly absence of community. But we can also glimpse an aesthetic community in the headlong rush to affirm one's ecstatic will in creation. The aesthetic promise of community does not establish definite and restrictive relationships between individuals, it creates and represents the intangible bond between the singular members of the community. When an unknown, nameless friend and I are captivated by a Van Gogh canvas, we are united in our contemplation beyond the impression the painting makes on either of us separately: I understand myself bound by an intangible bond to him, which remains unspoken as our eyes meet. A Shostakovich symphony, composed for unknown friends, binds together all of those unknown friends, those who have nothing in common, those who have yet to be born. The work of art is enveloped by the promise of community.

Perhaps it is a mistake to speak of a work of art; even the art publicly venerated by us in museums is not the result of a co-operative productive community, it did not originate from a shared common perspective, but from the excessive desire of visionaries to communicate, to seek the passion of their being outside of themselves. Art is the singular striving towards a "communal" representation of ecstatic desires, visions, dreams; it brings with it the aesthetic promise of community. This ecstatic aesthetic desire is the spring of defiant creation in the face of a world that will remain as stupid as it is impassive. Every occurrence of this ecstatic creative desire is an affirmation and confirmation of excess, a Nietzschean yes-saying to an infinitely renewed joy of creativity. It matters little that there is no created artwork, no tangible and enduring object, no relic of divine inspiration. Ultimately, we can conceive of every moment and every breath in the time of the aesthetic community as the boundless provider of and repository for such creations.

The writer, the artist seek to celebrate their ex-stasy as aesthetic communication, to lose themselves in this unrestrained movement towards nameless others, this gesture of friendship that rings without echo. Their absence of community constitutes the repository not of works of art but of the limits of artistic craving, the luminous diaries of Nijinsky or Van Gogh, the enveloping darkness of Rothko, Nietzsche in tears embracing the horse.

The Community of Lovers

For Nancy, lovers expose above all the unworking of the community[17]; their communication and kisses expose their communal self without fixing it, determining it, or defining it.

The other signifies for me in an excessive desire for communication and the desire to be challenged, to be contested. I am invited, as an unknown and anonymous friend, to partake in this passion. Singular beings represent a limit for each other; not the enclosing limit of absolute being, but the limit of ecstasy, of existing outside of oneself. We cannot go completely beyond ourselves to seek and found our own being in the passion of the other's being. Lovers desire this infinite passion, this complete dispossession of the self by the other. But the ecstatic desire for communication encounters as its limit, beyond comprehension, beyond silence, the abdication of the other's desire.

Lovers seek to liquefy their respective identity with every sigh, caress and explosion, to invent and fashion a fused identity. One enslaves oneself, with complete abandon, to the fantasies and nightmares of the other, to breathe with her, through her, only her.[18] This passion for the other is the passion for communication, community, or communion.

The absence of the community of lovers is not constituted solely by the burning passion of the ecstatic self to lose itself in an other, nor by the set of relationships we have all at one time maintained. The absence is constituted by the ephemeral solidarity which comes from the recognition and understanding of our ecstatic self as lovers, even though this lies beyond communication: love-affairs that resonate within us until death but that we cannot describe or communicate.

As artists and as lovers, we ex-statically seek to transcend ourselves in a doomed effort at community, a search without issue, which nevertheless inscribes absences of community on our passion.

The Community at the Threshold of Death

Ultimately, we require a witness to our dying, a hand, no longer therapeutic or efficacious, but which reassures: "I am here also." We come to the side of the dying one, knowing that there is nothing one can say, but that something should be said, that one has to find the strength for words, words for the dying.

Alphonso Lingis writes:

What can one say? Anything one tries to say sounds vacuous and absurd, in one's mouth.... There is, not in the words and the combinatory possibilities of language, the power to say what has to be said. Yet you have to be there, and you have to say something.... What is imperative is that you be there, and speak; what you say in the end hardly matters.[19]

Death dispossesses the dying one, envelops her in solitude, dissolves the bond of her dying hand, held in ours. We come to share the solitude of the death of the other, the loneliness of her radical dispossession.[20] The death of the other tears, ruptures, forecloses our evanescent common destiny; it reaffirms our loneliness. The dying one is already engaged in death, beyond recall, in a time outside of the time that was ours, shared, the time of her dying does not belong to the world; this world, now weary, no longer claims it.

The collapse of a world as the dying hand becomes weaker and fades, as death effaces the other, is the collapse of the world promised by the other, it is the disappearance of her affirmation of the world, of her creation of our shared world, of her desire to communicate her world. The world which subsists, again impassive and indifferent, no longer claims her time as its time, it no longer claims her ecstatic desire. But as my hand clasps the dying hand in a now futile gesture, I realize that her death is also my death, rehearsed, postponed, just as my death will rehearse and postpone still other's deaths. In this absence of community, I am an accomplice, a witness, giving testimony to this ephemeral bond.

While our death remains irrecuperably private, even within a community of warriors, our mortality outlines an absence of community. Our fragile absence of community consists of this intangible and unspoken bond, it is woven of our embodiment of the other's death.[21]

The Community of Those Who Have Nothing in Common

For Bataille and Blanchot, the exigency of community is most stri-
dent for those who have no community. Nancy, in the last lines of *The
Inoperative Community*, writes that he must think about the community
of those who cannot communicate, those who can neither read nor
write, or who have nothing in common. But, he remarks, in reality,
there is no such person.[22] Lingis, however, is overwhelmed by the exigency of community of those who have nothing in common: neither
language, culture, religion, nor projects, civil relations or social mores:

> We should have to find ourselves, or put ourselves in im-
> agination, in a situation at the farthest limit from kinship
> — in a situation in which one finds oneself in a country
> with which one's own is at war, among foreigners bound
> in a religion that one cannot believe or which excludes one,
> with whom one is engaged in no kind of productive or
> commercial dealings, who owe one nothing, who do not
> understand a word of one's language, who are far from
> one in age (for even being of the same age-group is a com-
> mitment) — and on whom one finds oneself completely de-
> pendent, for one's very life.[23]

Kinship of any kind produces ties, commitment, responsibilities, it
weaves a social fabric of exchanges, contracts, acknowledgements; it
defines civil duties, solidarity, family obligations. It is no longer possible to disengage a sense of identity from the multiple roles one per-
forms within one's own society, to assert a sense of self outside of that
which is defined by one's station, allegiances and actions.

And yet the passion for community is not satisfied by membership
in these pathetic groups, by communities based on rational calcula-
tion or societal ties. It is only when one has *nothing* in common that
one can face the other, naked, alone, and trust the piercing depth of

these eyes with one's life, with one's self, in a ritual of time im-
memorial. The bond that emerges then cannot be severed; it haunts us
for the rest of our lives. The true community fleetingly glimpsed
manifests itself as an absence. It cannot be maintained in a world
ruled by practices, exchanges, projects, obligations; it dissolves as
soon as one is re-integrated in the civilized social circus.

There is nothing but absence between us and those who have
nothing in common with us, no ground or reason to communicate our
ecstatic passions. And yet this absent community represents the limit
of community itself, the community of absent communities.

Absences of Community

The passion for community springs from our ecstatic desire for
the other, from our recognition that we cannot remain mired in immanence. The community cannot be invented, created or established
through our communal work or by congregating in communal
groups, even though the rhetoric of society or historical destiny would
have us believe so. Our passionate desire to go outside of ourselves
produces ecstatic art, makes us desire and love, and, confronted with
the limit of the other's death, makes us responsible accomplices. Our
rare encounters with those we have nothing in common with sudden-
ly makes us realize the absence of the community that we desperately
seek with our whole being.

By absences of community, we do not mean spaces from which
community has fled, from which it has absented itself; the community
is still to come. Rather, we indicate or point to a place where this absence is felt, which is haunted by the elusive promise of community.
The absences of community thus lie, however improbably, in the future, emerging from our passionate destiny.

Even though the community is still to come, it is not the outcome
of a historical process to which we passionately contribute, and will
not be realized. To apprehend and feel the absences of community, to

seek them in desolate places, is to understand that our passion for community makes the realization of a community our common but always postponed destiny. Our ecstatic passion is destined to remain unfulfilled; the passion for community is continuously aroused but never satisfied.

The absence of community is felt as a lack or privation only if we understand community as something that we have lost, and consider ourselves permanent exiles from a mythical or historical Eden. Many have objected to the use of the word "community" to name this community which is always still to come, seeking to reserve the word for possible communities of neighbours, kindred spirits, minority groups, or allies. Is it not humanity itself, rather than community, which Bataille, Nancy and Blanchot are trying to delineate or define here? Surely it is our humanity which makes us capable of creating art, loving others, respect death and those who have nothing in common with us.

And yet the four absences of community delineated here are much more than a definition of humanity; many other properties make us human. The absences of community craved by the ecstatic self constitute a desire for being-in-common with the other, a continuous flight from immanence. This passionate desire for being-in-common is a passion for community, but for a community still to come; for Nancy, a desire for communion; for Bataille, the notion of the sacred, the unleashing of passions. We have no community, but no-one is at leisure not to belong to the other's absence of community.

Blanchot concludes that one comes to expose one's solitude, one's loneliness at the *heart* of the community. The community, still to come, is not destined to cure us of or protect us from our solitude, but allows us to expose it.[24] Our ecstatic self passionately longs for absences of community, empty places to bury our ineradicable solitude.

Notes

1. An earlier version of this paper was presented at the Canadian Society for Hermeneutics and Postmodern Thought meeting at Carleton University, Ottawa, Canada, in June 1993; those present gave valuable and constructive criticism. The inspiration for the paper came from a seminar given by Alphonso Lingis at the Pennsylvania State University during Fall 1990. I also wish to thank Alphonso Lingis, Shawn Smith and Carl Collery for reading the manuscript and discussing it with me.

2. Georges Bataille, from *Contre toute attente*; quoted in Maurice Blanchot, *La Communauté Inavouable* (Paris: Minuit, 1983), p. 13. English translation by Pierre Joris: *The Unavowable Community* (Barrytown, NY: Station Hill Press, 1988). I have no quarrel with Joris' translation, but prefer to keep my own; page references are to the French edition.

3. Jean-Luc Nancy, "The inoperative community," trans. Peter Connor, in *The Inoperative Community*, ed. Peter Connor (Minneapolis: University of Minnesota Press, 1991), pp. 11-12.

4. Nancy, *The Inoperative Community*, p. 22; *ïnouï*, translated literally as "unheard," also means "unbelievable."

5. Georges Bataille; this quote is chosen by Blanchot as the epigraph of *La Communauté Inavouable*, p. 1, and taken up again on p. 45.

6. Quoted in Nancy, "The Inoperative Community," p. 1.

7. Maurice Blanchot quotes Edgar Morin: "Communism is the most important question and the principal experience of my life. I have never ceased to recognize myself in its aspirations and I still believe in the possibility of another society and another humanity" (*La Communauté Inavouable*, p. 10).

8. Blanchot writes: "… the deficiency of language that such words as *communism* or *community* seems to include [the root *common*] …" (*La Communauté Inavouable*, p. 9).

9. Blanchot, *La Communauté Inavouable*, p. 11.

10. "And for us the question of the community is henceforth inseparable from the question of ecstasy …" (Nancy, *The Inoperative Community*, p. 6).

11. Blanchot, *La Communauté Inavouable*, p. 16.

12. Yukio Mishima, *Sun and Steel*, trans. John Bester (Tokyo: Kodansha, 1970), p. 78.

13. The assessment in this paragraph is based on Nancy's own blurb for the French version of *The Inoperative Community*.

14. Despite the reasons advanced by Peter Connor, the translator of *La communaute désoeuvrée* (Nancy, *The Inoperative Community*, pp. xxxvi, 156), it is a mistake to translate "désoeuvrée" by "inoperative." I believe that "unworking," while still infelicitous, is a much better rendering of the original.

15. Nancy, *The Inoperative Community*, p. 32.

16. Bataille saw communication as constitutive of human reality, and ecstasy as "the bottomless depth of communication, which, without object, goes beyond knowledge" (quoted in Blanchot, *La Communauté Inavouable*, p. 34-35); Nancy

sees communication as an experience that constitutes our being (Nancy, *The Inoperative Community*, p. 19).

17. Nancy, *The Inoperative Community*, p. 40.

18. See the haunting novella by Marguerite Duras, *The Malady of Death*, trans. Barbara Bray (New York, Grove Press, 1986), to which Blanchot devotes the second half of *La Communauté Inavouable*.

19. Alphonso Lingis, *The Community of Those Who Have Nothing in Common* (Bloomington: Indiana University Press, 1994, p. 108.

20. Blanchot, *La Communauté Inavouable*, p. 21.

21. For Nancy, "the community is the presentation to its members of their mortal truth" (*The Inoperative Community*, p. 15; also quoted by Blanchot, *La Communauté Inavouable*, p. 24).

22. Nancy, *The Inoperative Community*, p. 42.

23. Lingis, *The Community of Those Who Have Nothing in Common*, pp. 157-158.

24. Blanchot, *La Communauté Inavouable*, p. 47.

3

Native by Nature?

Rick Harp

> *Let me pose the question clearly: If Indians are not to be
> considered victims of colonial aggression, how are we to be
> considered?…Why are we not considered as colonized by
> anyone other than ourselves? For any Indian, the questions are
> subjective and quotidian: How might I exist?*[1]
>
> > Jimmie Durham (Cherokee),
> > artist/activist

How might I exist, indeed? For me, a self-identifying Plains Cree —
whose passport reads "Canadian," whose first and (currently) only
language is English, whose mother is Native and whose father is not,
whose entire life has been spent in urban environments, and whose
education has been wholly obtained from non-Native institutions —
the question is as immediate and urgent as it is profound. And yet, as
critical as this question is, writing about it has proven to be no easy
task. Where to start? How to begin discussing what I feel to be central
to any serious consideration of "community" as it might apply to
Aboriginal peoples in Canada — the issues surrounding identity? For
me, thinking about these questions of community and identity seldom
occurs without simultaneously thinking of how they impact upon me
personally. And since my purpose here is to discuss how the politics of
identity have in fact served to undermine Aboriginal efforts at building community, what more immediate way to address the questions
facing Native peoples than to share with you some of my own? Now,
it perhaps goes without saying that my story is a "Native" one in so
far as it reflects, broadly speaking, the experiences of most Native
people. Yet, in a sense, that's part of the problem: for, despite some of
the vast cultural differences that exist between the various First Nations of this part of the continent, we are all known, and hence
treated, simply as "Indians." What we share, then, and what I wish to
discuss here, is how that locating or framing of our cultures, our lives
and most importantly our selves, has made it incredibly difficult to

know who we really are, and, therefore, what kind of community it is we seek to build.

Authentic Colonialism

It never ceases to amaze me how self-styled experts on Native peoples consistently fail to acknowledge the historical impact of colonialism on our lives, a relationship so antagonistic toward Indigenous peoples, it can only be described in terms of attempted (and in some cases, successful) genocide and ethnocide. And because this huge historical fact of colonialism is so key to understanding how we Native peoples got to where we are today, to attribute its omission by those-in-the-know-about-Indians to mere sloppiness reveals to me a fundamental mis-understanding about how colonialism works. Colonialism isn't just about the forcible acquisition of control over land and resources, it is also — perhaps even more so — about a particular way of knowing and relating to reality. What my limited academic work in this area suggests, what my lived experience tells me, is that not only has colonialism had a fundamentally pernicious impact on the way most members of the dominant Euro-Canadian society see and act toward Native peoples, but, more insidiously, on the way Native peoples look upon and act toward one another. It is that perception of ourselves and of our peoples which forms the bulk of my political and intellectual concerns.

"Who is a real Indian?": if there is one question which essentially captures the way in which Native identity is shaped by the forces of colonialism, this would be it. Moreover, it is the question to which many Native peoples have fought desperately among themselves to answer. And yet, sadly, at no point have enough of us stopped long enough to realize who is responsible for posing the question in the first place, never mind pondering whether or not an answer to it actually exists. Nonetheless, the query remains one Native peoples ask themselves everyday. I should know: I've asked it, both to myself and

to other Native people. We put this question to ourselves in a number of different ways, and through a variety of explicit and implicit means. And if, upon reading this essay, you remember only this question — *who is a* real *Indian?* — you will have learned one of the key methods by which a colonial society such as Canada operates to maintain itself: that is, through that time-honoured tactic of divide-and-conquer. Only in this case, what is being divided is epistemological as well as material in nature. A division, that is, between that which is *known* to be real and that which is *known* to be fake, between what is known to be authentically Indian, and that which, well, is anything but. The question which obviously comes to mind, then, is one which exists at the heart of every epistemology: how is it that we can say we have come to know this? In this case, the answer lies within the relations put in motion by colonialism itself.

Ultimately, Native peoples seeking to determine who they are independently of this non-Native discourse invariably encounter a dilemma, the essence of which Jimmie Durham captures perfectly:

> The world knows very well who we are, how we look, what we do, and what we say — from the narrative of the oppressor. The knowledge is false, but it is known. We [Native peoples], then, are left somewhere else (no-where else). By the very act of speaking, we contribute to the silence, the nullification laid upon us. It is not as though we ourselves are speaking from some pristine state of savage grace. Colonization is not external to the colonized, and it makes for neither wisdom nor charity among the colonized. Made to feel unreal, inauthentic, we often participate in our own oppression by assuming identities or attitudes within the colonial structure.[2]

Caught between being a readily understood "someone" and an unintelligible, invisible "no-one," the majority of Native individuals are forced to choose their poison. And it is when Aboriginal peoples feel compelled by their colonial condition to, in effect, internalize its discourse about who we are, that we embark on what can only be described as a form of institutionalized self-hatred.

The Purity of Colonialist Thought

To see how this discourse surrounding Aboriginality has come to be internalized by Aboriginal peoples, one need look no further than the "circumstances" of my birth. As I alluded to earlier, I am of what some might call "mixed" stock. What does that mean exactly, to say that I, as the son of a Native woman and a non-Native man, am of "mixed" blood? Here, the key word is blood. That's "blood" as in blood-lines and it is those blood-lines which mark off the so-called "real" Indians from the presumably fake kind. And so, if authenticity is the first principle animating colonial discourse (or, as I like to call it, discursive colonialism), then this concern with one's genes highlights the other closely-related principle, purity. Many times have I asked myself, or felt the need to be ready with a response to, questions about my parental lineage. But the genetics game is one Native peoples can never win. Never mind that genetic purity has existed nowhere on this Earth. By investing our sense of who we are in purely biological terms we run the real risk of ignoring the historical aspects of our being. To say that only other Indians should sleep with Indians simply ignores the enormous changes brought on by the historical processes of contact and colonialism, not to mention First Nations' historic willingness to bring non-Natives into their fold with little or no regard paid to the latter's race.[3] (In fact, strictly speaking, the category of *race* is not an *indigenous* concept at all but rather one which washed up on our shores with Europeans.) Thus, to label those Native individuals who choose non-Native partners as marrying "out" of their "tribe" only serves to uphold the colonialist viewpoint relying on such notions of purity.

I am reminded here of a comment made by Jimmie Durham, who once joked that he too is of mixed blood — that of his purely male father and his exclusively female mother. Yet, these seemingly ridiculous comments on Durham's part actually point to something quite serious, the reduction of Native identity to nothing more than one's DNA. But if who I am as an Aboriginal person is not merely a function of my gene pool, where are we to look to find the source of one's identity? I maintain that if our identities are to be seen as residing anywhere, it ought to be within our actions; in other words, within what we do, including how we do it. In speaking of his work with Native political groups, Jimmie Durham once declared that, in regards to the question of whether or not he is an authentic Indian, "the only sensible question would be, did I perform my jobs with integrity?" To which I add another: do my actions benefit the interests of Native people as a whole, or simply those of a chosen few? I'm thinking here of those members of the Indian elite class, the so-called Native representatives, who, in reality, serve the larger interests of the Canadian nation-state.

But what lies at the root of this identity insanity? Why has it come to occupy such a place of privilege among our so-called leaders? One of the major factors encouraging this genetically-based view of identity has been an ingenious federal invention known as "Status." A "Status Indian" is a purely political device created by the Canadian government which designates by law who is, and more importantly, who isn't, entitled to the "benefits" that Status confers. Such benefits (which are more accurately viewed as inadequate reparations for stolen land) include exemption from provincial taxes and funding for post-secondary education. "Non-Status Indians," on the other hand, are not entitled to such benefits. Yet, in spite of the inherent arbitrariness of Status, Status Indians have not joined together with non-Status Indians in trying to do away with it. Instead, non-Status Indians have spent much of their time and resources striving for the entitlements reserved for Status Indians. Meanwhile, Status Indians, eager to ensure that their access to federal funds is not threatened by the inclusion of non-Status Indians, do nothing. Obviously, the federal government has left itself in a position to simply play one group of Native peoples off the other. Proof of the effectiveness of this divisive strategy can be seen in Native peoples' actually organizing themselves along this designation into Status (most notably, the Assembly of First Nations) and Non-Status (including the Native Council of Canada) political groups.[4] Not surprisingly, these groups receive much of their funding directly from the federal government. Think about it: could there be a more apt or blatant symbol of our colonial condition than the fact that our sense of who we are has become contingent upon a legal definition we have had no part in creating?

As it happens, my mother is one of the many women who, in 1985, fought successfully to regain their Status, which they had lost for marrying non-Native men. For me, the return of my mother's Status meant that I was now entitled to Status as well. And to be quite frank, it was only at that point in my life that questions about who I am developed any sense of personal urgency. "Confirmed" and "legitimized" as I had then become by the conferring of this new Status (in both senses of the word), my previous low regard for any matters of identity had by this time been displaced by a need to know where I might fit in.

That need to fit in leads into a problem that I and many other "Bill C-31 babies" face when it comes to identifying as Native. The implication is that because I'm "part," because I speak English exclusively, and because I'm a pure-bred city-boy, my Native-ness is somehow in question. As if going off to live on my reserve is a simple matter of relocating. For while speaking my tongue and growing up in the company of my peers from birth are, in and of themselves eminently desirable, requiring them as necessary "proof" or evidence of my "Indian-ness" ignores the reality of reserve life; a life which, if I were to lead it, would likely see me: (a) extremely poor, by any one's standards; (b) demoralized beyond belief and (c) suicidal, if not already dead. Reserves, as a whole, are wastelands, and are so by design. Don't take my word for it: check it out for yourself, and I mean really check it out. Poverty, incest, abuse of all kinds, youth committing suicide at an epidemic rate: the reality speaks for itself.

We must refuse categorically to accept the notion that if you ain't home-grown, then you ain't the genuine article. For prior to contact, "home" was everywhere for Native peoples, not along some artificial East-West grid, and certainly not on some shitty little parcels of land like reserves. This apparent attachment to reserves on the part of some Native peoples is just another example of the way we've accepted if not embraced the boundaries others have laid out for us. Of course, with colonialism the situation is never quite that simple, but the fact remains that our future does not lie with reserves. The reason my mother left the reserve is because she knew, as did so many other Native people at that time, that if she, and, by extension, our peoples, were to survive, they would have to leave what remain unbelievably bleak environments. That's why she went to the city, and that's why I continue to live there. It is simply a matter of options: either live and eventually die out on the reserve or live in the city where you will have a fighting chance. Again, except for the rarest of reserves, "the rez" as originally conceived, will never provide the resources Aboriginal peoples require to foster any semblance of community.

And what of that community-building process? Here too, unfortunately, the debate among Native peoples over how we are to organize and govern our lives seems to have come down to being an either/or proposition: either you advocate a so-called "traditional" way of doing things or you buy into the "modern," presumably non-Native, way. In essence, this understanding of tradition accepts, if not embraces, the colonial view that in order for Native cultural practice to be genuine, it must demonstrate the strongest possible links to pre-contact Native society. In short, to be "traditional" is to adopt an utterly static view of Native culture. Given that the integrity of our identity as Native people does not rest solely within our genes but, more appropriately, in the way we conduct ourselves, to regard any and all change as "anti-traditional" is extremely problematic. Earlier, I commented about how the historical realities of contact and colonization have made the ideal of genetic purity impossible. It is essentially the same argument that I refer to here in dismissing the notion of cultural purity. The fact is, not only does this view assume that we have had no effect "back" on Euro-Canadian cultures, but, by its own logic, it makes any and all moves by Native people in a contemporary mode impossible. We are who we are today *because* we are historical beings, and efforts by Native people to keep things the way they were prior to contact only serves to legitimize colonial discourse about who we "really" are.

Ultimately, for any Native person in this society to know what it means to be "Indian" is to know precisely what, and who, we aren't. That is the paradox and the reality of Aboriginal existence today. But what to make of this realization, which, on its own, offers little in the way of practice? If it is true that we are only marginally better off for knowing that our identities as Native peoples lie both elsewhere and nowhere, what then? To be quite honest, I haven't a clue. Yet it is no small victory to realize that as one who occupies what can perhaps best be described as a contradictory position, courtesy of the contemporary forces of colonialism, that I am far from alone or unique. Hence, if anything is clear, it is that there is a need to push for an analysis and a politics which is capable of accommodating the contradictoriness and ambivalence of historical human existence, even if we can't yet envision what that politics might look like.

Indeed, what has come out most for me from this discussion is the realization that if any political strategy seeking to "go from here to there" is ever to succeed, it must recognize that while constraining categories, such as *race,* must be exposed as the lies they in fact are, the relations they simultaneously embody and engender are real, with real consequences for real people. In the Lorraine Hansberry play *Les Blancs,* a Black revolutionary named Tshembe marks the crucial difference between *race* as a device and the reality of its effects, conventionally known as racism:

> I believe in the recognition of devices as *devices* — but I also believe in the reality of those devices. In one century men choose to hide their conquests under religion, in another under race. So you and I may recognize the fraudulence of the device in both cases, but the fact remains that a man who has a sword run through him because he will not become a Moslem or Christian — or who is lynched in Mississippi or Zatembe because he is black — is suffering the utter reality of that device of conquest. And it is pointless to pretend that it doesn't *exist* — merely because it is a lie...[5]

The key to successful resistance will be grasping this difference between acknowledging the lie as a lie on the one hand, and moving beyond its categorical foundations on the other, all in the same subversive breath. Because, after all, people are not racist simply to piss you off. And while some of us may laugh at that last statement, in a sense, it has been the *de facto* organizing principle of our resistance. Instead of asking why people feel it might be in their best interests to be racist, intellectuals and political types content themselves with simply saying what it is, namely, something which "other," less-enlightened people come to believe in, not them. I am forced to draw this conclusion by what I see: intellectuals and politicos who, on their moral high-ground, continually overlook the contradictory position they take by mounting explicitly anti-racist struggles. For, in order for there to be anti-racism, one must accept that such a thing as *race* exists to begin as well. In other words, the problem isn't racism so much as it is believing the world is divided into races to begin with, and little in the way of existing praxis is designed to cope with this ambiguous state of affairs. It is only by looking more closely at the day-to-day reasons why people find racist attitudes appealing that the root causes of that symptomatic appeal, and what to do about them, can be ascertained.

Notes

1. Jimmie Durham, "Cowboys and ...," in *The State of Native America: Genocide, Colonization and Resistance,* ed. Annette Jaimes, South End Press, Boston, Massachusetts, 1992, p. 427.
2. Ibid., p. 423.
3. See, passim, James Axtell, *The Invasion Within: The Contest of Cultures in Colonial North America,* Oxford University Press, New York, 1985.
4. An excellent example of how the introduction of Status has led to much infighting among Native people is the current efforts by a group of Native women in the Canadian court system to regain the Status they lost in marrying non-Native men. Incidentally, this is not the case for Native men marrying non-Native women: in fact, the latter automatically *gain* Status. Again, it is ironic that any Native people find it desirable to fight for the recognition of an identity demonstrably inimicable to their interests. Or at least it would be ironic, if the reality of colonialism did not make survival impossible otherwise.
5. Lorraine Hansberry, *Les Blancs: The Collected Plays of Lorraine Hansberry,* ed. Robert Nemiroff, New York, Random House, 1972, in, bell hooks, *Black Looks: Race and Representation,* Between the Lines, Toronto, 1992, p. 27.

4

The Politics of 'Home'[1]

Anna Antonopoulos

> *I work more in India...but I find it troubling because I am In-*
> *dian; I mean, one would think that that would be a helpful thing,*
> *but I don't find it a helpful thing. I'd much rather it wasn't my*
> *so-called 'home'.*[2]

Elsewhere I have argued that the historical transformation that gives rise to the modernist vision of 'home' as the utopian and sheltered place of safety for which we supposedly all yearn, draws upon an exclusionary, territorializing, xenophobic, premodern and patriarchal cult of 'home' that predates and prefixes it.[3] My study of the religious, legal, literary, and philosophical records of the past reveals a powerful tradition located at the time of Greek and Roman Antiquity and organized around the secretive, furtive, and dark cult of the 'home' or the *hestia*. Historical, sociological, phenomenological and anthropological studies on the sacred hearth in classical Antiquity conducted by the French Annales school (Philippe Ariès, Fustel de Coulanges, Jean-Pierre Vernant, Marcel Detienne, Louis Gernet, Jean-Joseph Goux) reveal the presence of a repressed symbolic void at the very centre of our signifying fields[4] — a void that not only produced a discourse and an experience of 'home' in ambiguous, ambivalent, and contradictory terms, but one that was deeply tied to an atavistic and patriarchal abjection of the female body which it has since repressed, neutralized, naturalized and at the same time reproduced. This opens the door to more detailed investigations of the implications and possibilities of a psycho-historical approach to culture which would apply the techniques of psychoanalysis to both collective popular rep-

resentations in Antiquity and to their movement through the paths of
history. I take the recent post-structuralist interest in the *chora*[5] as one
such move that could yield productive results in disengaging 'home'
(hestia) from a number of other related terms, for example, the chora
(country), on the one hand, and the *oikos* (household), on the other. It
also allows for a more critical perspective on how popular cultural
representations may work to fill the gap between academic and
"revolutionary" practices in ways that foreclose the opportunity of
"productive crisis" between them.

Bringing It All Back 'Home'

To put the matter squarely: the 'home' is back. When I undertook
to write an interdisciplinary Ph.D. dissertation on the 'home' more
than five years ago, I considered my work pioneering in terms of
bringing attention to the discursive circulation of a term that had yet
to be identified as such. Today, if there is a buzzword in cultural critique, the word is 'home'. The discourse on 'home' is in the air
everywhere.[6]

Throughout the last number of years increasing attention has
been given to the 'home' in special issues of such diverse forums as
New Formations (no. 17, 1992, special issue "The Question of 'Home'"),
Social Research (vol. 58, 1, 1991, "Home: A Place in the World," ed. Stan-
ley Cavell), *Architecture and Behavior* (no. 5, 1989, special issue
"Phenomenological Aspects of the Home").

In particular, recent years have seen a boom in the discursive circulation of 'home' in relation to questions of identity and community.
'Home' as homestead and as homeland has emerged as something of a
nodal point (*foyer*) in questions ranging from race, ethnicity, and
nationalism, to sex, gender, and desire. From modernism and
postmodernism, to debates about colonialism, sexuality, gender, race,
class and a host of others, 'home' — and by extension 'home'stead and
'home'land — are tied to unresolvable controversies. Caught between

the deconstructive demand of a postmodern sensibility that relativizes 'home' as a provisional and unstable space and the recuperative needs of a reactionary or emancipatory nationalism such as that of the New Right, the New Traditionalism and a host of others, contemporary theoretical practices are held in tension as the 'home' becomes a site of struggle for competing discourses. From lamentations about the "loss of home" to its redefinition in seemingly new and radical ways, the discursive management of crises (from those about sex and gender identity to others about the often irresolvable impasses of race and ethnic struggles) of the base term 'home', continues to assume the aspect of an unproblematic geographical location — a container of problems and problematics, rather than a problematic category in itself.

In light of this proliferation of discourses and seemingly unresolvable debates that have swept over academic practice in the course of the last five to ten years, I want to focus (by way of example) on how this fixing of the 'home' as pre-given turns upon one aspect of academic crisis-management: the management of a crisis about gender. The outcome of my position will be that a fixing of 'home' as a stable, homogeneous and bounded space upon which to make identitarian claims about community instantiates the management (i.e. the sealing over) of an unease about gender that we cannot afford to overlook if we are to take seriously the relationship between academic and revolutionary practices as outlined above. I will begin by addressing this fixing, this imaginary unity that attends the base term 'home', as a *catachresis* — in Spivak's own catachrestical sense of "a word for which there is no adequate referent"[7] — that first cropped up in the discourses of postmodernism and media studies. While these are not historically "first" to either fix the 'home' or to manage crises about gender,[8] I take them as my point of departure in so far as they are the first to identify these processes discursively as the rhetorical and epistemological site of a dissolution of imaginary unity and of stability, thereby instantiating a far-reaching strategy of academic crisis-management that takes 'home' as its own vanishing point.

'Home' in the Discourses of Media Studies and Postmodernism

The discourses of contemporary media studies suggest the emergence of what Daniel Czitrom calls a "new community,"[9] Marshall McLuhan a "global village,"[10] and Raymond Williams a new "home-centered way of living."[11] In these discussions about today's technological society, the 'home' achieves the value of a site at which conventional polarities between 'private' and 'public', the 'domestic' and the 'social', the 'outer' worlds of mobility and transience and the 'inner' realms of a fixed internal world, no longer hold. As a consequence, the 'home' gains a key place in theorizing questions of identity and community in relation to social change. However, while some celebrate this proclaimed dissolution of traditional bounds, others fear the loss of real community, the loss of 'home', or of a "sense of place"[12] within social reality.

Joshua Meyrowitz, critical analyst of the electronic age and its effects upon social behavior writes that as 'home' becomes a less "bounded and unique environment," the walls of the family 'home' no longer present "effective barriers" that can work to isolate the family from the larger community and society.[13] In an equally apocalyptic vein, there are those theorists for whom this alleged dissolution of bounds takes the frightening form of a "collapse" of public life as the new social value that is placed on the individual, privatized, nuclear 'home' announces the disintegration of community and human identity. For these theorists of doom, community "disintegrates" into the 'home', which then becomes the last bastion of social life. This disintegration in turn "threatens" to extend into marriage, at which point the 'home' itself risks becoming an anachronism. It is then further supposed that when this happens, we are looking upon the loss of the very foundations of our humaneness.[14]

The 'home' marks a rhetorical as well as theoretical site for the development of discourses on the subject of postmodernism as well.

For Baudrillard, it is the space of "the social"; for Grossberg, the space of "the self"; and for Arthur Kroker, that of "the body." As post-modernity invades and liquidates one inner sanctum ('home') after another body, self and private life become inscribed with the rhetoric of hyper-space — dissolution, mobility, hyperreality. In each case, the postmodernists' discourses of the late 1980s depend upon the imagery of a mass-mediated cybernetic world and lend a new rhetorical twist to communication technology's investment and colonizations of domestic space documented by contemporary media studies.[15]

Thus, Jean Baudrillard's essay "The ecstasy of communication"[16] constructs 'home' as a satellite-world, a micro-cosmic universe televisually turned macro. In this essay, Baudrillard sets up 'home' as the theoretical site for a postmodernist challenge to the oppositions 'public'/'private' in a reading of the "end of the social." Following the lines of his initial critique of television economy as form of object- or commodity-fetishism,[17] Baudrillard here turns his critical (postmoder-nist) eye to this economy as a "means of communication."[18] As such, it is the "obscene delirium of communication" — a state of "negative ecstasy," "fascination and vertigo" in which the classical dichotomies of space and place, of interior and exterior, and of private and public, are transformed by "an original and profound mutation of the very forms of perception and pleasure."[19] This "mutation," achieved through the "electronic encephalization" of the environment,[20] is ex-pressed by Baudrillard in domestic terms. Triggered by the "private telematics" of the domestic television screen and its images, it is "the passage into orbit of our private sphere itself"; the "elevation of the domestic universe to a spatial power" and a "spatial metaphor"; and, the "realization of a living satellite, *in vivo* in a quotidian space."[21]

As a testimony to the final dissolution of the classical epis-temological and ontological dichotomy between public and private space in the electronic age of the postmodern, the screen image in Baudrillard's text stands supreme as it "explodes the scene formerly preserved by the minimal separation of public and private."[22] In perhaps no other form have the boundaries that separate, classify, limit, and delimit space and place been so radically challenged as they are here, in what Baudrillard calls "this forced extroversion of all interiority" and "forced injection of all exteriority" that "the categorical imperative of communication literally signifies."[23] And yet, if "this explodes the scene formerly preserved by the minimal separation of public and private,"[24] it is not because it has been challenged from without. In Baudrillard's reading of the electronic age, the *locus principus* of postmodernity is the "domestic universe,"[25] itself, as "the entire universe comes to unfold arbitrarily on your domestic screen" and the "most intimate processes of our life become the virtual feeding ground of the media."[26] In this discourse, the domestic universe of the 'home' becomes the key site for Baudrillard's proclamation of "the end of the social."[27]. In the glare of postmodernity's television era, this domestic "universe" heralds the "extermination of interstitial and protective spaces"[28] as well the "loss of public space,"[29] and "forms a sort of ecological niche where ... opacity, resistance or the secrecy of a single term can lead to catastrophe"[30] and where pleasures are "aleatory and psychotropic."[31]

Lawrence Grossberg's discussion of the "affective economy of television" posits an affective mobility of 'home' as subjective space for the "nomadic" subjectivity of today's electronically-equipped self. Where for Baudrillard the site of the postmodern 'home' marked the dissolution of the opposition between public and private spaces, for Lawrence Grossberg the 'home' is a site that refigures the dualism between the mobility and fixity, or fixed situatedness. Grossberg takes 'home' as the *in situ* paradigm for travels in the postmodern. In his essay "The in-difference of television: mapping TV's affective economy,"[32] and in a conference paper "Mapping cultural audiences: cultural practices and nomadic subjects,"[33] Grossberg grafts 'home' onto the very structure of postmodern subjectivity. Addressing the omnipresence of the television image, Grossberg departs from a hermeneutics of domestic space to embark instead upon a hermeneutics of the billboard as the model for postmodernist theory. "Television's economy," he writes, "is a domestic one, built upon structures of security and comfort." However, he adds, "TV is a domestic medium but it need not constantly domesticate every image; nor is it already domesticated, without any role in ongoing cultural struggles."[34] Working off the dual aspect of television as both a domestic medium and a domestic object, Grossberg proceeds to leave behind the TV object's "fixed" location within the field of enclosed domesticity in order to address the vagrant and migratory nature of the practices of "reading" the TV medium and its images.[35]

In mapping out television's "affective economy,"[36] Grossberg sites a new paradigm of domesticity, a paradigm that rests with the theory of the subject itself — in this case, a postmodernist and "posthumanist theory of the subject"[37] that invokes the notion of a "nomadic subjectivity," whose subject, "the nomad" is itself a "site of struggle, an ongoing site of articulation with its own history."[38] Thus, for Grossberg, the postmodern subject is "amoeba-like," "struggling to win some space for itself in its local context." Rejecting the theory of the unified "existential subject" as well as the poststructural deconstructionist theory of the "fractured" and "fragmented" one,[40] Grossberg proposes to locate postmodern subjectivity in the "nomadic wandering through ever-changing positions and apparatuses" that constitutes the "complex set of practices and identities" of the TV audience.[41] In view of the fact that "any individual position is actually mobilely situated in a fluid context," Grossberg develops the image of a "nomadic subjectivity,"[43] in the context of a hermeneutics not of the domestic television image itself, but of the highway billboard. With the model of the "billboard" as roadmarker "to be driven past," Grossberg proposes to read the self reading the television image.[44] By contrast, with the fixed audience-position of reading "texts to be interpreted," Grossberg's metaphorical billboards engage the mobility of the hermeneutical subject and his reading project.

However, if the billboards are indeed "a space in which many different discourses ... appear,"[45] this is merely a space within a space;
for this "nomadic relation to the media"[46] is but a secondary relation,
and the "wandering nomad," a home-body. In this respect,
Grossberg's metaphorics of the postmodern locate the site of what he
calls the "complex social spaces of media effects"[47] within a double-ar-
ticulation of the 'home'-image: first, the residential home of the
television medium (or object), and second, the subjective (metaphysical) 'home' of the subject — nomad. Significantly, Grossberg's
nomadic subject is not living a metaphysical "homelessness" either
within himself or his domestic environment. For Grossberg the
nomad's 'home' resides in the space within himself, and with its own
effective articulation as a "shape": "while its shape is always determined by its nomadic articulations, it [the nomad] always has a shape
which is itself effective."[48] Indeed, "moving along different vectors
and changing its shape, but always having a shape,"[49] this, according
to Grossberg, is a subjectivity that is "always at 'home'."[50] In this in-
stance, it may be said that the 'home' as the dominant image of
postmodernity is mapped across a space significantly more fluid than
the circumscribed hemispheres of the domestic household universe.

For Arthur Kroker, the "disappearing body" in hyper-modernity
becomes the rhetorical lieu for the *mise-en-abîme* of a disappearing car-
nal 'home' as postmodernism's technological imperative colonizes the
inner sanctum of the very site of "authenticity" and "the real": cor-
poreal interiority. In his apocalyptic tale of the body as the kaleido-
scopic site of a grand simulacrum, Kroker domesticates the image of
the "hyperreal." From the site of telematics, of television's cybernetic
revolution, and of "computers as the externalization of memory," and
"*in vitro* fertilization as the alienation of wombs," Kroker rewrites the
myth of the prison-house of the soul as a fantasy of the body's ruins,
as the postmodern "body" becomes the locus of just one more rhetoric
field: what Kroker finally calls "a fantastic simulacra of body
rhetorics."[51] For as Kroker provocatively contends, under the "fin-de-

millenium" sign of the "hyperreal," "the body no longer exists."[52] Thus, in Kroker's postmodernist tract, it is body that announces the disappearance of 'home'. In his essay "Theses on the disappearing body in the hyper-modern condition,"[53] Kroker engages in a discourse that casts the myth of place and space in the ever-fading light of a vanishing ideal. Thus he writes: "its dissolution into a semiurgy of floating body parts reveals that *we* are being processed through a media scene consisting of our own (exteriorized) body organs in the form of second-order simulacra."[54] In this way, Kroker launches the final *coup-de-grace* to the *ex-nihilo* site of the 'home' in a vision of the dying gasp of a body-without-organs and a site-without-a-seer.

As much as their work is a reflection upon changing historical and technological realities that may effect radical changes in our perceptions of ourselves and our domestic universe, as well as a reflection upon changing epistemological currents that take as their model the spatialization (versus the temporalization) of theoretical categories,[55] the 'home' in these postmodernist theorists of the *domus* is, as Meaghan Morris points out in her readings of 'home' in postmodern theorists of travel, "a space which is blank."[56] Not only does this "blankness" mark the denial of situatedness in the social, and the erasure of social, political and theoretical struggle, but also, the potential of a concept of 'home' for the articulation and analysis of political categories and practices is thus vaporized.

However much the 'home' is cited/sighted/sited as the new paradigm of social existence, subjectivity, and the body, in media and postmodernist discourses, it is never acknowledged as the site of the reproduction of gender: i.e. as a gendered space and the site of our situatedness in the social. For 'home' is not only a complex fantasy space of conflicting wishes, desires, and experiences for both women and men, it is at the same time a marker of the social and structural changes within the family.[57] The erasure of this aspect of the 'home' as the site where the position of women and the articulation of gender has been so ideologically and historically inscribed, is a significant absence in the "packaging" of 'home' in the discourses of postmodernism and media studies and is particularly problematic when we consider the implications of 'home' in relation to questions of identity and community. In order to appreciate the difficulties, or even understand the stakes, it is necessary to first dip into a different set of discourses — discourses that, besides being affected by the "new domesticity," also have something to do with bringing it about.

'Home' and the Feminist Politics of Location

Concerned with examining the nature of patriarchal (versus simply capitalistic) structures of dominance, feminists such Adrienne Rich, Dorothy Dinnerstein, Nancy Hartsock, Nancy Chodorow, and Betty Friedan (to name but a few) point to the domestic arena as a key site for the application of gendered power and consequently as the ideal point for its reversal. In her celebrated "Notes toward a Politics of Location"[58] Adrienne Rich describes the impact of late twentieth-century feminism as one which demonstrates the fact that "wherever people are struggling against subjection, the specific subjection of women, through our location ... has to be addressed." Against Virginia Woolf's stirring passage from *Three Guineas* that proclaims that "as a woman, I have no country. As a woman I want no country. As a woman my country is the whole world,"[59] Rich's discourse invests 'home' with the value of a ground.

As grounds from which to speak, the bounded place of our location — read as 'home', 'body', 'sex', or 'nation' — materializes a space within which not only the history of technology but the history of gender is permanently and indelibly inscribed. "Technologies of gender" abound as much as those of labour, entertainment, and information, as the locale of the 'home'. 'Home', like 'body', 'sex', 'woman' and a host of other subjugated terms, resurges as the chief locus of a newly politicized discourse on domesticity, a discourse that not only

marks the historic subject of feminism, but the female subject —
feminine body, gendered subjectivity, and woman's entrance and
"situatedness" in the social, as well. Across Rich's ever-widening
ground of "location," or situatedness within bodies, subjectivities, and
social realities, the 'home' as that space in which the position of
women is both structurally and culturally inscribed becomes a principal ground and an unequivocal centre for the articulation and
theorization of the projects of feminist theory and feminist politics.
Struggling against the use of lofty and privileged abstraction, and
pushing to name and locate the grounds from which we speak as well
as the criteria by which claims of knowledge are legitimized, Rich
gives voice to a feminist "politics of location" that emphasizes "place"
as a position within social and epistemological reality.

However, as much as Rich's feminist push for a politics that takes
'home' as its political location can aid in assessing current descriptions
of 'home' in the technological age, others remind us to stay vigilant
about positing 'home' as a fixed and stable or homogeneous space,
working to erode the notion of 'home' as an unproblematic
geographical location. Thus from within feminist practice we might
ask, as Meaghan Morris does in her own celebrated essay "At Henry
Parks' Motel," what happens to the idea of 'home' as "woman's place"
when 'home', rather than the voyage, is rewritten "as chaos and fragmentation, labour, transience, 'lag' — or in quite different terms …."[60]

Postmodernist dislocations of 'home' mean that 'home' cannot be
posited as a stable homogeneous site but as a site of intersecting and
mobile social and discursive spaces, bodies, and subjectivities. They
also mean recognizing the ways in which economic and technological
change in the 1980s — what Haraway has called, following Richard
Gordon, "the homework economy"[61] — has equally been transforming family life;[62] and it is in the disjunction between the postmodern
rhetorics of displacement, instability, mobility, and transience, and the
feminist insistence on the importance of "place" in critiques of
everyday life[63] that a politics of 'home' emerges as a ground upon

which productive crisis between academic and non-academic practices can be achieved. As bell hooks writes: "once woman-centred space exists, it can be maintained only if women remain convinced it is the only place where they can be self-realized and free."[64]

And it is worth pointing out that the stability of 'home' is not always posited by feminist theory in binary opposition to a postmodernist accent on travel and mobility. Even more basic is its presence as the securing of a freedom from dread, horror, fear, contamination, even as it reproduces it. Feminist theorists have also shown how, in the space of domesticity, relations of care and connection are laced with experiences of coercive domination, whether it be domination of parent over child, or male over female. As bell hooks notes, it is in "this convergence of two contradictory impulses" — the impulse to dominate and violate together with that to care for and nourish — that the 'home' provides "a practical setting for feminist critique, resistance, and transformation."[65]

In this context, it is a question of "developing a vigilance for systematic appropriations of a *differential* that is one basis of exchange into the networks of the cultural politics of class- or gender-*identification*."[66] One of these "systematic appropriations" that calls for vigilance is that of the space of the 'home' by the entertainment media.

Heimlich Horrors and *Unheimlich* Homes in the Media

In the last few years, cinema and TV have hit 'home' with a vengeance. Television viewers across Canada and the U.S., for example, are being nourished with a steady diet of Sunday evening premiers in which images of domestic violence, horror and suspense, brought by American national television to my cozy *heimlich* livingroom space, bathed "a kinder, gentler America" in family blood: children killing parents, husbands killing wives, wives killing husbands and babies, babies killing babies — not too different from the prime-time news, the local newspapers, or the wave of B-grade movies of the 90s (*War of the Roses, The Hand That Rocks the Cradle, Single White Female, Fatal Attraction, Basic Instinct, Body of Evidence,* for example). The family home, once private haven-in-a-heartless-world, is now the public space of a shared hell-on-earth: a black and scary communal pit into which the families of Sunday-night prime-time viewing across Canada, Québec, and the U.S. are indiscriminately pitched. To expedientially bring biography and geography to crisis, I have to say that I, of course, was not one of *them.* I was studying the twisted moorings of the American mind and its producers: "I" being "whole," un/American, and single. Yet, even though I do not have a "family" in the traditional sense, am part of an other-than American community, and have little sense of a national identity, watching these comfortable livingroom horror-pictures gave me a curious sense of (be)longing. A family-in-ruins supposes a family to be ruined; a free country, the ties that bind; a community, the rudiments of imagination.

Taken together with the anachronization of the family, marriage, and the 'home', and the breakdown of a binary thinking that polarizes men and women, work and play, sexes and nations, these popular representations of the family 'home' stand as a break with the binary opposition between the public and the private; which opposition, relegating violence to the worlds of men and public life and women to the nurturing peaceful families, is long gone. However, in the use of highly controlled, staged, and domesticated settings for producing these effects of uncontrollability, as for example in the *Oprah* show,[67] these documentations serve to re-inscribe our belief in the presence of the bounds marked out by 'home' and not-'home'. In the domestication of violence and crisis, their message supposes that nothing much has changed at the same time as it knows that nobody would be viewing if it had.

While American docudramas about incest, child and wife abuse, domestic violence, rape and murder seem to be recognizing the 'home' as a gendered space of power and domination, the belief (need, desire) that they should support community makes these popular representations of domestic violence serve the utopian ideal of the 'home' as a kinder and gentler woman's sphere of freedom and safety. Taken together with the centrality of questions of the *heim* or 'home' to issues of nationalism, sexuality and identity, these representations lend a new slant to the Freudian topic of repression, and by necessity, also to its history.

The *Herkunft* of 'Home'

In his famous essay *"Das Unheimlich,"* translated by Strachey as "The 'Uncanny'," [68] Freud provides powerful etymological proof of the double meaning of 'home' as the site of both the familiar and the strange. Drawing on the notion of sexual repression to explain how the *heimlich*, meaning "homey," "known," "familiar," produces as a synonymn its own opposite: i.e. the *unheimlich*, meaning the strange, dreaded, secret, and feared, Freud observed that the uncanny or *unheimlich* "is nothing else than a hidden, familiar thing that has undergone repression and then emerged from it." [69] Relying upon the testimonies of male patients who claimed that they felt there to be something uncanny about the female genitals, what emerges from this repression is the ambiguous position of the female body — at once the ultimate *"unheimlich* place" and the entrance to "the former *heim* (home) of all human beings." [70]

As Angelika Bammer says in the introduction to a recent issue of *New Formations* [71] devoted entirely to the contemporary question of 'home': "on all levels and in all places, it seems, 'home' in the traditional sense (whether taken to mean 'family' or 'community', or 'homeland'/'nation') is either disintegrating or being radically redefined." [72] In current etymological and discursive extensions of 'home' as 'home'stead and 'home'land, the 'home' and by association the unitary ideals of family, nation, community and identity all emerge as provisional, inherently relative and unstable spaces and are absorbed by the uncanny euphemysticism of postmodern speech, in which identities are "local authenticities," 'homes' are "transient settings" and nationalisms the interstitial space in which these "meet and merge."[73] In this absorption of the double meanings of 'home' in the all too familiar yet ever stranger turns of postmodern phrase, *heims* nevertheless continue to circulate free of all sexual determinism, sexual memory, or even sexual amnesia.

In the unheimlich language of the moving image, homes have horrors, and one of its horrors is still sex. We have not significantly strayed from the Freudian model. The famous essay has not collected dust either. Following Freud one might convincingly argue that the modernist mystification of *heim* as *heimat* — a mystification that produces 'home' as the universal site of a utopian (be)longing — has today been repressed in the service of a decidedly postmodernist sensibility only to resurface in the feminist one.

I have so far looked at this foreclosure as it is guaranteed by certain media representations of the 'home' — representations in which 'home' as the quotidien site of gendered horror, and violence and dread work to seal over a crisis about the presence of gender in the 'home'. My argument has been that if we take the ambiguous position of the 'home' as site of a doubled meaning, then the place to be occupied by a sexualized community — a gendered "national popular," so to speak — becomes extremely uncertain. Insinuating itself as the space between the 'home'stead and the 'home'land, such a space occupies the vanishing point of a signifying system on the basis of which heterogeneous spaces have long ceased to present themselves as such. Michel Foucault, who single-handedly mapped out the spaces of hospitals, prisons, asylums, and the like, was nevertheless the one to point out that "the space in which we live, which draws us out of ourselves, in which the erosion of our lives, our time and our history occurs, the space that claws and knaws at us, is also, in itself, a heterogeneous space. In other words, we do not live in a kind of void."[74] In this "heterogeneous" space, a naturalized and nationalized dream of identity and community unfolds which fixes that space in ways that prohibit productivity and social change.

A'Home' By Any Other Name

I want to end my discussion with a personal anecdote which animates the defining terms of the above. I will begin by making some observations about the politics of the name as they are played out in questions where 'home' as the metaphor for identity and community is based upon its reference to the absence of a name.

I recently had the opportunity to reflect on 'home' as the theoretical ground for a feminist politics of location at a philosophy conference in Boston, where I and a few other "Canadian" feminist philosophers were thrust into discursive anonymity for the lack of an authorized discursive place from which to speak. While the topic in question was ostensibly the (post-structuralist) problematic of gender, it became clear as discussion progressed that the "gender" in question had, as its political ground, the particular racial or national status of its interlocutors. Discussion quickly crystallized around American (i.e. United States) post-structuralist feminism on the one hand — replete with references to the cultural politics of the (at the time) Bush Administration — and, on the other, racialized critiques from the margins. In the words of Eve Sedgwick, who seems to have had a similar conference experience, "the term 'America' had come, unbidden and unremarked, to occupy a definitional centre for almost every single one of the papers, and for the conference as a whole, in a way that no one could even seem to make visible enough to question."[75] "American" Queer met "American" Black with the silenced voice of the American Chicanos piping up to defeat the standstill. To cite Spivak, "that is what the audience wanted to hear: a voice from the margin."[76] It was in this fight or flight for marginality that those who were completely out of the picture were us: a small handful of Canadian feminists who dared not speak the unspeakable. "Canada" as cultural identity did not seem to cut it as the "name" for anything.

I will not dwell on documented insights into Canada's "vegetable imagination,"[77] nor contest some well-meaning attempts to inscribe this flatland with the lure and promise of a discourse on gender.[78] Nor will I dwell on the fact that for others, this imaginary "Canadianness" can be summed up by a local-specific philosophical experience of Nietzschian *ressentiment* — a *ressentiment* arguably born out of the u-biquitous imperialism of our American neighbours, on the one hand, and the colonial forces of French and British domination, on the other.[79] For it appeared to me, at that moment of speechlessness, that I could formulate my/our geopolitical ground, our/my politics of loca-tion, in precisely the absence of a name. As Northrop Frye has so sug-gestively noted: "Canadian sensibility has been profoundly disturbed, not so much by our famous problem of identity ... as by a series of paradoxes in what confronts that identity ... less the question 'Who am I?' than ... some such riddle as 'Where is here?'."[80] Unfortunately, the value of this utterance as forcing the politics of identity into productive crisis has somewhere gotten lost.

For this statement is not to be confused with just another varia-tion of the "As Canadian as (Blank)" syndrome, a syndrome that a number of theorists have used to point to the vacuousness of "Canadian" as a cultural identity. Frye's utterance is, I submit, at the heart of the absence of a clear, indivisible, homogeneous, unam-biguous, and totalizing referent for such identity. As that ground from which to speak a politic — one pertinent to feminist practices (both academic and revolutionary) in general and relevant to contemporary questions of identity and community in particular — 'home' becomes a site that is pliable and, to use Kristeva's language, fundamentally "catastrophic."[81] In this respect, what I think comes forth in Frye's remark is the sense in which the *unheimlich* feeling experienced here is symptomatic of the absolute indeterminateness of 'home'. This feeling is, in Frye's case, much less a reflection of what Michel de Certeau calls a feeling of *hors de chez soi* (a feeling compatible with a postmodernist nomadic-style position) as it is a feeling and an experience of being *"étrangers à l'intérieur même"*.[82] From the point of view of the absence of a constitutive outside (*un dehors*) as a position (in language, or culture) from which to look upon this situation of *"étrangeté chez soi,"* de Certeau has himself concluded that we have no recourse but to bump up continuously against the limits (*buter contre ses limites*) of this foreignness-at-home and proposes this "bumping up" as the actual blueprint for proceeding with cultural studies (*science de l'ordinaire*) of any sort.[83]

Reading further into Julia Kristeva in light of this "Canadian" predicament of disorientation and radical homelessness, one is struck with a similar obsession with place and displacement characteristic of the state of radical abjection *"Au lieu de s'interroger sur son 'être', il* (the abject) *s'interroger sur sa place: "Où suis-je?" plutôt que "Qui suis-je?".*[84] In *Strangers to Ourselves*,[85] Kristeva describes this phenomenology of foreignness — this not-at-home-like feeling — in the formation of nation-states. She writes:

> It is perhaps on the basis of that contemporary individualism's subversion, beginning with the moment when the citizen-individual ceases to consider himself as unitary and glorious but discovers his incoherences and abysses, in short his "strangeness" — that the question arises again: no longer that of welcoming the foreigner within a system that obliterates him but of promoting the togetherness of those foreigners that we all recognize ourselves to be.[86]

In this way, the very title 'home' as the name of that "strangeness" and "outsiderness" acts as its own "vanishing point" as it were. However, this is so only to the extent that 'home' presents itself in discourse as a stable, fixed and homogeneous ground for theorizing identity and community, a ground depicted on the basis of a radical separation between the inside/outside, the 'home' and the "not-home." Its failure (in the case of abjection and Canadianness-à-la-Northrop-Frye-et-al.) to univocally and unequivocally name a location that is fixed and bounded by this 'home'/not-'home' opposition produces a crisis both in relation to what has emerged as the problem of the intellectuals in Canada as well as in relation to the kinds of practices that might "fix" a feminist politics of 'home': the absence of a recognizable name to denote its marginality. The problematic nature of defining the local specificity of Canadian thought, as of "Canadianness" in general,[87] and which emerges in the face of doing feminist theory "in the Canadian context," shifts the ground upon which to locate a feminist politics. As a revolutionary practice it must now stand in the spaces of what Simon Harel so aptly names, in his discussion of Montréal as a ground from which to write and speak, the "*hors-lieu.*"[88] The difficulty, in this case, of establishing "my 'home'" as bounded, fixed and name-able ground from which to speak, makes palpable to me the kinds of catachresis that 'home' as the name of such a ground supposes.

'Home' Free: Outside in the Domestic Machine

Following Biddy Martin and Chandra Talpade Mohanty who, in their insightful essay "Feminist Politics: What's Home Got to Do with It?," point to the importance of the "problematics of home" as the search for ways to conceptualize community differently without dismissing its appeal, we might envisage the possibility of "a new sense of community which gives up the desire for the kind of 'home' where the suppression of difference underwrites familial identity";[89] one in which it is the unsettling of bounds that accompanies a rela-tional notion of identity displacing the notion of a "fixed" centre. In this context, it is in the disjunctions between the postmodernist rhetorics of the displacement and instability, mobility, and tran-sience and the feminist insistence on recognizing the importance of "place" in critiques of everyday life,[90] that 'home' (h̶o̶m̶e̶) emerges in its full force as a ground upon which to reconceptualize political community; conceptualize that is, the relations between 'home', identity and political change.[91] In its articulation with the feminist push for a politics of location, the emergence of 'home' as key rhetorical/theoretical space in academic discourse drives a wedge between the traditional search for a secure place from which to speak, and "the awareness of the price at which secure places are bought," the awareness of the exclusions, omissions and the limits of such a place.[92]

In this wedge driven between 'home' as a stable and protected place, and 'home' as the basis for exclusion, the political stakes of the equation of home/community/identity emerge. While it does not erase the desire for unity and for comm-unity, this is a wedge that disrupts, destabilizes, and undercuts it. Re-created through the struggles and contradictions of the everyday, 'home' (h̶o̶m̶e̶) as paradigm for political community becomes, in this reading, reconceptualized as unstable, contextual, relational; the object of struggle, and always the product of interpretation and history. Implicating the individual in contradiction, this realization that 'home', 'unity', 'stability', 'sameness' — interpersonal as well as political — is fragmentary, does not however preclude agency.[93] On the contrary, it restores meaning to the subjects of the gendered body, the construction and negotiations of gendered subjectivity and the transformation of the social: without erasing its political significance.

Keeping in mind that 'home' designates nothing but "the invisible and only apparently self-evident boundaries around that which we define as our own," I only hope to have prompted some rethinking of this aporia at the heart of our concerns about identity and community and pointed to new ways for engaging with 'home' (h̶o̶m̶e̶) without dismissing its importance and appeal as a concept and a desire. One can envisage the end to the longstanding Western "politics of home" at the base of contemporary discourses of domestic space in favour of an epistemology of cultural, societal and fantasy spaces that takes into account the experiences of women in lived social and political contexts. Thus to maintain, after Morris and others, the theoretical necessity of neither abandoning nor too obsessively clinging to the conventional equivalence of woman and the 'home',[94] it is necessary above all to return to its roots, revisit its history, and rethink its meaning: prize open this equivalence at the very heart of its inception.

Notes

1. Besides forming the subject matter of my dissertation, the ideas outlined herein have been presented in forums of various sorts including the Canadian Society for Women in Philosophy, the Canadian Society for Hermeneutics and Postmodern Thought, the Canadian Studies Association, the Canadian Women Studies Association, the Canadian Aesthetics Society, the Ontario Philosophical Association, the Canadian Philosophical Association. I want to thank Geraldine Finn, Morney Joy and the Society for Hermeneutics and Postmodern Thought for giving these ideas a warm and generous space in which to grow. Thanks also to Sandra Bartky, Liz Grosz and to Pat Smart for supportive comments that spin off these ideas in new and exciting ways.
2. Spivak 1990, 49.
3. For a full discussion of the historical development of a fixed discourse on 'home' in the history of Western intellectual development, see my unpublished dissertation *The Space That Claws and Knaws: Topoi of a Critical Discourse on 'Home'* (Antonopoulos 1992).
4. Goux 1984.
5. Kristeva 1984; Derrida 1987; Grosz 1993; Butler 1993.
6. Cavell 1990; Barbey 1989; Seamon 1990; Harman 1989; Luxton et al. 1990; Rybczynski 1986.
7. Spivak 1993, 298, no.3
8. See my article "The Double Meaning of *Hestia*: Gender, Spirituality, and Signification in Greek Antiquity," *Women and Language* 16, 1 (1993): 1-6.
9. Czitrom 1982, 91ff.
10. McLuhan 1964, 20.
11. Williams 1975, 26.
12. Meyrowitz 1985.
13. Meyrowitz 1985, vii.
14. Seamon 1987, 12; Harries 1983, 20.
15. Morley 1986.
16. Baudrillard 1983a.

17.   Baudrillard 1981, 53-57.
18.   cf. Ibid., 54.
19.   Baudrillard 1983a, 132.
20.   Ibid., 129.
21.   Ibid., 128.
22.   Ibid., 130
23.   Ibid., 132.
24.   Ibid., 138.
25.   Ibid., 128.
26.   Ibid., 130.
27.   Beaudrillard 1983b.
28.   Ibid., 131.
29.   Ibid., 130.
30.   Ibid., 128.
31.   Ibid., 132.
32.   Grossberg 1987.
33.   Grossberg 1988.
34.   Grossberg 1987, 45.
35.   Ibid., 45.
36.   Ibid., 41.
37.   Ibid., 38.
38.   Ibid., 39.
39.   Ibid., 39.
40.   Ibid., 38-39.
41.   Ibid., 38.
42.   Ibid., 38.
43.   Ibid., 38.
44.   Ibid., 31.
45.   Ibid., 31.
46.   Ibid., 38.
47.   Ibid., 38.
48.   Ibid., 39.
49.   Grossberg 1987, 38.
50.   Grossberg 1988.
51.   Grossberg 1987, 22.
52.   Ibid., 20.
53.   Ibid.
54.   Ibid., 21.
55.   Stephanson 1988, 6-7.
56.   Morris 1988a, 12.
57.   Kuhn 1978; Barrett, 1980.
58.   Rich 1986.
59.   Woolf 1977, 109.
60.   Morris 1988a, 12.
61.   Haraway 1990, 208.
62.   Nicholson 1990, Haraway 1990.

63. Morris 1988a, 43; 1988b, 194.
64. hooks 1984, 27.
65. hooks 1989, 21.
66. Spivak 1993, 63.
67. Probyn 1993.
68. Freud 1958.
69. Ibid., 153.
70. Ibid.
71. Bammer 1992.
72. Ibid., viii.
73. Clifford 1988, cited in Bammer 1992, vii.
74. Foucault 1986, 23.
75. Sedgwick 1992, 235.
76. Spivak 1993, 55.
77. Frye 1971, i.
78. Smart 1993.
79. Dorland 1988.
80. Frye 1971, 220.
81. Kristeva 1980, 17.
82. de Certeau 1990, 29.
83. Ibid., 29.
84. Kristeva 1980, 15.
85. Kristeva 1991.
86. Ibid., 2-3.
87. Harcourt, cited in 1992.
88. Harel 1993, 389ff, 401.
89. Martin and Mohanty 1986, 205.
90. Morris 1988a, 43; Morris 1988b, 194.
91. Martin and Mohanty, 192.
92. Ibid., 206.
93. Ibid, 209.
94. Ibid., 191.

References

Antonopoulos, Anna. 1992. *The Space That Claws and Knaws: Topoi of a Critical Discourse on 'Home'*. Ph.D. Dissertation, Concordia University, Montreal.

Antonopoulos, Anna. 1993. "The Double Meaning of *Hestia*: Gender, Spirituality, and Signification in Antiquity." *Women and Language*, 16, 1 (Spring): 1-6.

Bammer, Angelika. 1992. "Introduction." *New Formations*, 17.

Barbey, Gilles, ed. 1989. *Phenomenological Aspects of the Home*. Special Issue of *Architecture and Behaviour* 5, 1: 1-84.

Barrett, Michèle. 1980. *Women's Oppression Today: Problems in Marxist Feminist Analysis*. London: Villiers Publications Ltd.

Baudrillard, Jean. 1983a. "The ecstasy of communication." In *The Anti-Aesthetic*, ed. Hal Foster. Washington: Bay Press, 126-134.

Baudrillard, Jean. 1983b. *In the Shadow of the Silent Majorities … Or the End of the Social and Other Essays*, trans. Paul Foss, Paul Patton and John Johnston. New York: Semiotext(e).

Baudrillard, Jean. 1981. *For A Critique of the Political Economy of the Sign*, trans. Charles Levin. St. Louis: Telos Press.

Butler, Judith. 1993. *Bodies That Matter: On the Discursive Limits of "Sex."* New York: Routledge.

Cavell, S. ed. 1991. *Home: A Place in the World*. Special Issue of *Social Research* (Spring).

Czitrom, Daniel. 1982. *Media and the American Mind: From Morse to McLuhan*. Chapel Hill: University of North Carolina.

de Certeau, Michel. 1990. *L'invention du quotidien 1; arts de faire*. Paris: Gallimard.

Derrida, Jacques. 1987. "Chora." In *Poikilia: Études offertes à Jean-Pierre Vernant*. Paris: EHESS.

Dorland, Michael. 1992. "Mathew Arnold in Canada: The Lonely Discourse of J. Peter Harcourt." In *Responses: In Honour of Peter Harcourt*, eds. Blaine Allan, Michael Dorland, Zuzana M. Pick. Montreal: The Responsability Press.

Dorland, Michael. 1988. "A Thoroughly Hidden Country: *Ressentiment* in Canadian Culture." *Frenzy: The Canadian Journal of Political and Social Theory* 12, 1-2: 130-164.

Foucault, Michel. 1986. "Of Other Spaces." *Diacritics* 16 (Spring): 22-27.

Foucault, Michel. 1977. *Language, Counter-Memory, Practice: Selected Essays and Interviews by Michel Foucault*, ed. Donald F. Bouchard. Ithaca: Cornell University Press.

Freud, Sigmund. 1958. "The 'Uncanny'." In *On Creativity and the Unconscious*. New York: Harper and Row.

Frye, Northrop. 1971. *The Bush Garden: Essays on the Canadian Imagination*. Toronto, Anansi.

Goux, Jean-Joseph. 1984. "Vesta, ou le sanctuaire de l'être." *L'interdit de le représentation*. Colloque de Montpellier. Paris: Seuil.

Grossberg, Lawrence. 1988. "Mapping popular audiences: cultural practices and nomadic subjects." Unpublished paper presented at the multidisciplinary conference Rethinking the Subject in Discourse. March 18-20. Montreal: McGill University.

Grossberg, Lawrence. 1987. "The in-difference of television: mapping TV's affective economy." *Screen* 28, 2: 28-45.

Grosz, Elizabeth. 1993. "Women, Chora, Dwelling." Unpublished paper presented to the Society for Phenomenology and Existential Philosophy, New Orleans.

Haraway, Donna. 1985. 1990. "A Manifesto for Cyborgs: Science, Technology, and Socialist Feminism in the 1980s." In *Feminism/Postmodernism*, ed. Linda J. Nicholson. New York: Routledge.

Harel, Simon. 1992. "La parole orpheline de l'écrivain migrant." In *Montréal Imaginaire: Ville et littérature*, eds. Pierre Nepveu and Gilles Marcotte. Montreal: Fides.

Harman, Lesley D. 1989. *When A Hostel Becomes A Home: Experiences of Women*. Toronto: Garamond.

Harries, K. 1983. "Thoughts on a non-arbitrary architecture." *Perspecta* 20: 9-20.

hooks, bell. 1989. *Talking Back: Thinking feminist, thinking black*. Boston: South End Press.

hooks, bell. 1984. *Feminist Theory: From Margin to Centre*. Boston: South End Press.

Kristeva, Julia. 1991. *Strangers to Ourselves*. Trans. Leon S. Roudiez. New York: Columbia University Press.

Kristeva, Julia. 1984. "The semiotic *Chora* Ordering the Drives." In *Revolution in Poetic Language*. New York: Columbia University Press.

Kristeva, Julia. 1980. *Pouvoirs de l'horreur*. Paris: Seuil.

Kroker, Arthur. 1987. "Theses on the disappearing body in the hyper-modern condition." In *Body Invaders: Panic Sex in America*, eds. Arthur Kroker and Marilouise Kroker. Montreal: New World Perspectives.

Kroker, Arthur and David Cook. 1986. *The Postmodern Scene: Excremental Culture and Hyper-Aesthetics*. Montreal: New World Perspectives.

Kroker, Arthur. 1985. *Feminism Now. Canadian Journal of Political and Social Theory* 9, 1-2.

Kuhn, Annette, and Ann Marie Wolpe. 1978. *Feminism and Materialism: Women and Modes of Production*. London: Routledge.

Luxton, Meg, Harriet Rosenberg, and Sedef Arat-Koc. 1990. *Through the Kitchen Window: The Politics of Home and Family*. Toronto: Garamond.

Martin, Biddy, and Chandra Talpade Mohanty. 1986. "Feminist politics: what's home got to do with it?" In *Feminist Studies/Critical Studies*, ed. Teresa de Lauretis. Bloomington: Indiana University Press. 191-212.

McLuhan, Marshall. 1964. *Understanding Media: The Extensions of Man*. New York: McGraw-Hill.

Meyrowitz, Joshua. 1985. *No Sense of Place: The Impact of Electronic Media on Social Behavior*. Oxford: Oxford University Press.

Morley, David. 1986. *Family Television: Cultural Power and Domestic Leisure*. London: Comedia.

Morris, Meaghan. 1988a. "At Henry Parkes Motel." *Cultural Studies* 2, 1 (January): 1-47.

Morris, Meaghan. 1988b. "Things To Do With Shopping Centers." In *Grafts: Feminist Cultural Criticism*, ed. Susan Sheridan. London: Verso. 193-226.

Probyn, Elspeth. 1993. "Television's *Unheimlich* Home." In *The Politics of Everyday Fear*, ed. Brian Massumi. Minneapolis: University of Minnesota Press.

Rich, Adrienne. 1986. "Notes toward a Politics of Location." *Blood, Bread, and Poetry: Selected Prose 1979-1985*. New York: Norton.

Seamon, David. 1987. "Phenomenology and Environment — Behavior Research." In *Advances in Environment, Behavior, and Design* 1, eds. Ervin H. Zube and Gary T. Moore. New York: Plenum.

Seamon, David, ed. 1990. *Environmental and Architectural Phenomenology: Newsletter*, 1, 1 (Winter).

Sedgwick, Eve Kosofsky. 1992. "Nationalisms and Sexualities in the Age of Wilde." In *Nationalisms and Sexualities*, eds. Parker, Andrew, Mary Russo, Doris Sommer, and Patricia Yeager. New York: Routledge.

Smart, Patricia. 1992. "The (In?)Compatibility of gender and Nation in Canadian and Québécois Feminist Writing." Unpublished paper presented at the Association for Canadian Studies conference on "Theoretical Discourses in the Canadian Intellectual Tradition," St-Jovite, Québec.

Spivak, Gayatri Chakravorty. 1993. *Outside in the teaching Machine*. New York: Routledge.

Spivak, Gayatri Chakravorty. 1990. *The Post-Colonial Critic*, ed. Sarah Harasym. New York: Routledge.

Spivak, Gayatri Chakravorty. 1988. "Can the Subaltern Speak?" In *Marxism and the Interpretation of Culture*, eds. Cary Nelson and Lawrence Grossberg. Urbana: University of Illinois Press.

Spivak, Gayatri Chakravorty. 1983. "Displacement and the Discourse of Woman." In *Displacement: Derrida and After*, ed. Mark Krupnick. Bloomington: Indiana University Press.

Stephanson, Anders. 1988. "Regarding Postmodernism — A Conversation with Fredric Jameson." In *Universal Abandon? The Politics of Postmodernism*, ed. Andrew Ross. Minneapolis: University of Minnesota Press.

Williams, Raymond. 1975. *Television: Technology and Cultural Form*. New York: Schoken.

Woolf, Virginia. 1977. *Three Guineas*. London: Hogarth.

5

Mommy Dearest: Women's Studies and the Search for Identity

Sonja Embree

You'll take a map, of course, and keep it
open in front of you on the dashboard,
though it won't help. Oh, it'll give mileages,
boundary lines, names, that sort of thing,
but there are places yet
where names are powerless
and what you are entering
is like the silence words get lost in
after they've been spoken.

It's the same with the highways.
The terse, comforting numbers
and the sign that anyone can read.
They won't be any good to you now.
And it's not that kind of confidence
you're after anyway.

What you're looking for are the narrower,
unpaved roads that have become
the country they travel over, dreamlike
as the spare farms you catch
in the corner of your eye,
only to lose them
when you turn your head. The curves

that happen without warning
like a change of heart,
as if, after all these journeys,
the road were still feeling
its way through.

excerpt from "Into The Midst Of It" by Bronwen Wallace [1]

Let me begin by telling you a little bit about myself and how it is that I have made my way to this page. I recently completed an undergraduate degree in Women's Studies and Anthropology at Carleton University in Ottawa, Canada. During my studies, I was an active member of my Women's Studies programme: for three years, I sat on both its management committee and its steering committee; I spent one year with the student advisory committee for the joint chair in Women's Studies; during my third year, I was employed directly by the Institute of Women's Studies to set-up a small resource library; and, in my final year, I was awarded a teaching assistant position for two sessions of the introductory course. My participation in these various activities was both intellectually and emotionally challenging, and it provided me with valuable insight into Women's Studies as a programme/department in terms of the position it occupies within the academic institution, and the way in which it attempts to affect positive change in both the university setting as a whole, as well as in members of its student body.

During the last two years of my degree, however, I found myself feeling increasingly ambivalent and disillusioned with my studies. This must come as a surprise given the extent of my involvement with the programme, and the fact that I feel lucky to have met and worked with many wonderful women as either fellow students or professors. Yet, when I came across the above passage by Bronwen Wallace, her vivid description of the contrast between a highway and a country road reminded me of my Women's Studies programme. For it is like a highway with "terse numbers" and "signs that anyone can read," while the kind of confidence I am looking for can, perhaps, only be found on "narrower, unpaved roads." Oh, it will give names, statistics, theories and goals, but these are not enough since "there are places yet" where these things are powerless and which are incapable of filling "the silence words get lost in." Women's Studies has become rather like a map which is kept open on the dashboard for full viewing, but which I seem incapable of reading. Why do I feel this way, and how did it come to be? This question is not an easy one to answer; in fact, I have discovered that much reflection was needed in order to provide not only an adequate response, but a truly honest one. What I would like to do with the following paper is to outline some of the insights I have made, for I feel that in addressing my ambivalence and disillusionment regarding the programme, my intellectual travels might be illuminating with respect to feminism in general and Women's Studies in particular.

Initially, I assumed that my troubles were related to the criticisms which the programme was/is receiving that did not place it in a very positive light. The attacks which the Western feminist movement[2] is undergoing for its re/production of a predominantly white, middle-class, heterosexist, able-bodied perspective on women's issues are also being directed against Women's Studies programmes in terms of course content, staffing, and institutional elitism. For example, Himani Bannerji and Linda Carty address the systemic racism and the "tokenism" they have experienced in Unsettling Relations: the university as a site of feminist struggle.[3] Punam Khosla, a community activist, describes feminist academia as a "leech" which "uses people from the 'real' world as specimens" in order to carry out its work, thereby creating and/or reinforcing a hierarchy of power relations between women.[4] Kathleen Martindale has identified the institutional and cultural homophobia of Women's Studies classes manifested primarily through "absences, silences, failures and exclusions."[5] And

Christina Sommers has come to regard Women's Studies as "a dys-
functional family with too much emphasis on hugs and 'touchy-feely'
issues."[6]

Reading these criticisms made me feel very uncomfortable and I
knew that some of them were applicable to my programme since the
student "grapevine" indicated that others were dissatisfied. What is
happening? I asked myself. Isn't Women's Studies supposed to be the
new, progressive, and anti-discriminatory discipline which strives to
liberate both student and professor alike? Earlier literature which ex-
amined the role and purpose of Women's Studies had, for the most
part, a positive tone: its ideals were considered progressive, the expectations were high, and praise was abundant. In such works as
Theories of Women's Studies, edited by Gloria Bowles and Renate
Duelli-Klein,[7] Marguerite Andersen's "Empowerment Through
Women's Studies,"[8] and "Feminism and Women's Studies in the
Academy," written by Vivian P. Makosky and Michele A. Paludi,[9] the
programme is variously described as a space where "the deconstruction of sexist myths which women often internalize on a deep personal level" can occur safely through the facilitation of "the
expression of both the intellectual and emotional realm";[10] as "a forum
for empowering women within academic settings by making them
visible, validating their perspectives and experiences, and providing
them with a voice for articulating their concerns";[11] and, in terms of
the broader feminist movement outside the university, Women's
Studies "implies profound change in the structure of knowledge, the
university, and society ... [acting] as an instrument or weapon ... to
mobilize women for political action."[12]

Despite my ambivalence, I nevertheless tend to agree with these
claims. In taking Women's Studies courses, I learned about the various
forms and manifestations of oppression which women experience and
I was provided with some ideas of how I, myself, might be able to help
in working for change; by recounting the accomplishments of women
normally made invisible by traditional practices of history, the

programme expanded my own sense of what I might achieve, based on the energy and determination of strong role models; because of its interdisciplinary nature, I was able to explore disciplines I otherwise would have ignored such as religion, music, and law; and finally, I learned how to think critically and to question theories and modes of knowledge presented as "natural" and/or as "truth."

I think it is important to point out however, that I am white, middle-class, heterosexual and able-bodied; that the experiences which I enjoyed during the course of my degree stemmed from, and were influenced by, these various privileges; and that some of my peers who were not thus privileged were not as willing to declare a similar level of comfort. In fact, of the most commonly held criticisms heard through the student "grapevine," were homophobia and racism, and these are two forms of discrimination of which I, myself, have not been victim. So where was my discomfort and ambivalence coming from? After all, if anyone is to be at home and happy, it should be me, given that the structure and content of the programme are ones which purportedly cater to my background and interests. As I continued to reflect upon my research into and my experience of Women's Studies, I came to see that what has continually prevented me from fully embracing my studies is best described as a sense of alienation. And psychoanalytic theory rather than empirical research has helped me to see where that alienation was located.

In her article, "Sexual Politics and Psychoanalysis: Some notes on their relation," Rosalind Coward discusses the value of using psychoanalysis as a tool to better understand the way in which our culture's sexual hierarchy continues to reproduce itself despite the best efforts of the feminist movement. One of her points is that,

> the claim made by psychoanalysis is that what is spoken, what is exchanged in everyday forms of speech and behaviour and in systems of representation within society, are only half the story. Conscious behaviour, thought, and

> expressions are only the tip of an iceberg. They are com-
> promises formed between unconscious desires and social
> necessities.[13]

Thus, quite often the kind of subjects we become and the truths to which we submit are processes that unfold quite literally beyond our control; the effects of such processes, however, have considerable influence and should not, therefore, go unexamined. For example, in terms of feminism and the struggle for women's equality, greater acknowledgement needs to be given to the fact that "simply" removing certain societal barriers and forms of discrimination will not necessarily lead to a woman's complete liberation. What I mean by this is that pursuing ideal social conditions may very well lead to improvements in the external lives of women (i.e. material well-being), but it might not necessarily satisfy any of the internal (i.e. emotional) needs and/or desires which they may have. Furthermore, it could be argued that, in some instances, these needs and desires have a more direct influence on the way in which day-to-day thoughts, feelings, and behaviour are organized and experienced, and that the presence of oppressive material conditions may not fully account for any existing grievous subjective experiences.

Referring to Freud's hypothesis that identity is precarious, Coward describes subjectivity in the following manner:

> "I" am no longer a coherent, conscious, rational being. This
> "I" is only the product of choices not taken, desires not ful-
> filled and conflicts not expressed. But these elements are al-
> ways likely to return, to disturb and surprise.[14]

If the repetition of thought and behaviour patterns in the unconscious constitutes — at least in part — our subjectivity by shaping individual perspectives used to view and, therefore, participate in life, then perhaps it is worthwhile to investigate the way in which unconscious thought processes work to position an individual in relation to the feminist movement in general, and to Women's Studies in particular. To what extent are my feelings of alienation from my studies a result of past subjective experiences which continue "to return, to disturb and surprise"?

While describing her childhood experiences of playing the piano, Susan Heald uses the term "fraudulent" because, although she was competent and could play well, she did not regard herself as especially talented or creative as so many others did. She states that this sense of fraudulence occurred because "I did not really occupy the subject position ... as it was defined for me."[15] During my years in Women's Studies, there were several occasions when I too felt fraudulent because I found it difficult, if not impossible, to apply what I was learning to my own lived experience, and subsequently felt "unfeminist" in terms of my position as a Women's Studies student and as a follower of the women's movement in general. In fact, I became increasingly aware that, in terms of fighting the oppression of women, I was not as devoted as I thought I "should" have been. Certainly there were times when I felt despair over and complete revulsion at the treatment so many women have undergone, and I have gone through stages where I thought that all men should be blasted from the earth. However, I am sorry to say, that the full force of my anger had been, and continues to be, primarily directed at my mother.

For as long as I can remember I have alternately held feelings of hatred or fear of my mother as a result of the physical and emotional abuse she meted out on a daily basis to me and my two sisters. From the moment we awoke in the early morning until our heads hit our pillows at night, we girls lived a life of regiment and discipline. Almost every minute of every hour was filled with activities and chores such as piano lessons, ballet lessons, flute lessons, German lessons, extra school work on top of regular homework assignments, gymnastic lessons, housework, and tasks to be done out in the garden. Our house was quite large with expansive front- and back-yards, and my mother was always able to find some aspect in need of attention no matter how small or trivial. She was an extreme perfectionist and everything had to measure up to her high standards ... from the tidiness of our desk drawers, to the eradication of every last weed from the lawn; from the "correct" placing of a window curtain to the marks we achieved at school, nothing was left untouched. To an outsider, my family had the appearance of being quite successful. We had a beautiful home, a nice car, my father was a well-regarded neurologist, and my mother sewed beautiful clothes and nurtured a lavish greenhouse and abundant rock garden. And, of course, my sisters and I were extremely well-behaved. What very few people were aware of, however, was that not to be well-behaved, resulted in much physical and emotional abuse from my mother. Thus, we girls lived life on the edge, so to speak, jumping at every wish and command barked out at us and doing our very best to please her in order to escape her temper.

Our determined efforts, alas, were sometimes thwarted by natural childish inclinations, and our accompanying "failure" was met with disapproval and forms of punishment which were intended to teach us a lesson we would surely not forget. I must point out that our "sins" were not of a serious nature, but consisted more of such trifles as losing a button from a coat, mistakenly letting the dog run loose from its leash, or getting a cavity in one's tooth. Most of these occurrences were beyond our control, but for some reason my mother could not grasp this and, instead, she dealt with such incidents by beating us furiously.

As the years passed, my mother's style of discipline grew more severe, a factor which I attribute to her awareness that, as our bodies grew bigger and stronger, her power to control and discipline us would diminish. Thus, her sense of frustration with this reality provoked her to act in unforgivable ways: she would chase us with knives; she once knocked the wind out of my eldest sister with a severe blow to her back; she force-fed my middle sister the vomit which she had just expelled due to extreme nervousness; and she beat me once continuously for several hours because I had lost a screwdriver. During this time, my father was at work, setting up his doctor's practice which required him to put in very long hours, including weekends. That old phrase, "wait 'till your father gets home," did not apply in my family because at the first sight of his car coming up the driveway, the feeling that my sisters and I generally experienced was that of relief.

When I was eight, my mother began to experience insomnia and periods of severe depression, and she started to see a psychiatrist who prescribed her various medications. Her authoritative ruling subsided somewhat as she began to spend more and more days in bed. Finally, after a suicide attempt, she was hospitalized and I regret to say that in the two years she was gone, I experienced some of the freest moments of my life. Later, when she returned home, I felt rather sorry for her because I could see that she was faced with significant shifts in terms of her position within the family, and her marriage to my father was quite obviously under strain. In a very sad way, she must have felt like a stranger in her own house. Within six months, my father had moved out and by the end of the year, both my sisters had left and moved in with him. Thus, I was left alone with my mother and remained so for the following two years, whereupon she was re-hospitalized and I went to live with my father. Despite the relatively short time span of those two years, during which I was eleven and twelve years old, they had a deep effect on me and continue to do so now, some fourteen years later.

Thus, in terms of my sense of alienation as a student, it is clear to me now that this is derived from being born of and mothered by a woman whose presence I have always disliked and for whom I have come to hold little respect. How is it possible to join hands with other women and fight the "oppressor" when I shudder at the thought of having to even touch the woman who was, to me, oppressive? How can I rant and rave about the exclusion of women from positions of authority, privilege and power, about the physical and mental abuse of women, about the lack of dignity and respect accorded to women when I am willing to show only some small element of warmth to the woman who gave birth to me and who fed, clothed and nurtured me for the first twelve years of my life? Granted, feminist theory has, without a doubt, softened my attitude towards my mother in terms of being able to empathize with some of the issues she has had to face. But it has not been able to persuade me to change my behaviour towards her. No matter how much feminist analysis I take in about violence in the home, about the cycle of violence in our society, about the oppressive nature of the institution of motherhood, etc., it cannot alleviate the pain which I experienced; pain which was inflicted upon me not at the hands of a man, but at those of a woman.

I would like to introduce here the term, "bifurcated consciousness" which sociologist Dorothy Smith used to describe her experience of academic training. Smith discovered that the conceptually ordered world of intellectual thought which she needed to carry out sociological research was fundamentally removed from her local and particular world of raising two children in which emotional and physical nurturing took precedence. She describes this "split" as

> two modes of consciousness that could not coexist with one another. In practice of course they "existed' in the same person, often in the same places, and certainly they often competed with one another for time. But moving from one to the other was a real shift, involving a different organization of memory, attention, relevances and objectives, and indeed different presences.[16]

In terms of my own position and attitude towards Women's Studies, I too struggled with a "bifurcated consciousness": as a student, I was able to participate in the intellectual world of feminist theorizing and administrative processes on the one hand, but my "other" local and particular world of guilt and anger, which is organized and influenced by past subjective experiences of my mother, produced in me a second "domestic" mode of consciousness which, like Smith's, "competed" with the first for time. My own mother, in fact, unknowingly commented on this "split," when, after hearing what my academic major was, she retorted: "How can you be in Women's Studies when you ignore the most important woman in your life?" Quite so.

The point which I hope to make clear here is that women differ not only in terms of their material conditions, physical appearance, sexual orientation, religious affiliation, age, etc., but also in terms of their (former) subjective experiences, and these subjective experiences can be as significant a factor in organizing one's lived reality. For example, my white, heterosexual, middle-class, able-bodied being can in no way erase the values which my mother taught me about women, myself, and life in general, values which are inextricably bound up with the way in which I positioned myself as a student of Women's Studies and as a feminist. This last point prompts me to conclude that feminism's goal of establishing a mass-based, unified movement is an impossible ideal since each woman carries with her her own unique unconscious desires and needs, and it is therefore unreasonable to expect that she will be able to identify with and/or support every so-called "feminist" issue. Likewise, Women's Studies itself should accept the fact that it will neither achieve perfect "sisterhood" since it is unrealistic to assume that a single political interest (i.e. feminism) or a single course of study (i.e. Women's Studies) will guarantee any sense of solidarity, shared understanding, or feelings of inclusiveness among women. No programme, regardless of its mandate, is capable of fully addressing the expectations of the unconscious mind.

For many feminists, the futility involved in trying to recruit all women for battle is surely a hard pill to swallow; however, perhaps the very existence of this futility allows for an alternative understanding to the meaning of feminism as a social movement and of Women's Studies as an academic discipline. If I, upon self-examination, discover the real nature of my feelings towards my choice of studies (i.e. ambivalence), then I am forced to question my motives for enroling in such a programme in the first place ... what was I looking for when I signed up? What did I hope to achieve both personally and academically? Furthermore, how would other students respond to these questions, and could a similar type of enquiry be applied to members of the feminist movement in general? For some women, living in a sexist world and the struggles which this entails is reason enough to justify the development of a feminist consciousness. In fact, anger towards men could, in itself, be an organizing tool. However, I wish to also entertain the possibility that both the feminist movement and Women's Studies may offer women something which only the desires and needs of the unconscious are able to recognize and appreciate; more precisely, these desires and needs concern the feelings of inclusiveness and shared understanding to which I referred above, and not necessarily the (explicit) goal of the "liberation" or advancement of women. In an otherwise alienating society, feminism might act as a type of "community," providing women with a sense of security and sanity which is missing from other parts of their lives. And with respect to feminism within the university setting, perhaps it is the "mini-community" of Women's Studies which offers this same set of "services" to its female students.

My intent, here, is not to "blame" women and accuse them of being blind or naive if they are perchance supportive of feminism and/or enrolled in a Women's Studies programme. Rather, I am interested in speculating upon what it is that makes these so appealing. As Patricia Eliot has pointed out, the "point is to not eliminate desire, rather to recognize that we are subject to it in ways that often escape us and that subvert our conscious intentions."[17] I think that in terms of my own situation, being exposed to a compassionate "female" medium which advocated "making [me] ... visible, validating [my] ... perspectives and experiences, and providing [me] ... with a voice for articulating [my] ... concerns,"[18] provided me with the comfortable mothering that I lacked and which I continue to crave at times today.

Now, I do not wish to presume that all students enrolled in Women's Studies are embarked upon a journey in search of their lost mothers; however, I will make the assertion that the programme provides some form or sense of belonging (i.e. a community) which members use, in one way or another, in the shaping of their own identities. For example, a student in one of my discussion groups said to me after class one day, "Thank God for this course [Introduction to Women's Studies] because all of my other ones made me feel like I was a number, and here the prof and the T.A. made me feel like I was human."[19] This student did, indeed, feel like a human since she had — like all other Women's Studies students — been taught that the programme is a "different" discipline since its goal is to function on a more personal basis. And who would not agree that it is a far better feeling to be dealt with as a human than as a mere number?

I have actually come to regard Women's Studies as the "good mother" of academia, for despite its various flaws, it is likely one of the few disciplines which attempts to take into consideration such commonly ignored issues as the inseparability of the intellectual and emotional realms of both its students and individuals in general; the reality of the differences among women in terms of race, sexuality, socio-economic standing, age, physical ability, etc.; and the power which professors possess in their role as teacher and its possible effect. Occupying this role, however, does not necessarily guarantee carefree and unproblematic circumstances, for it requires much time, physical and emotional energy, and patience (much like the real mothering of a child) on the part of those professors and administrators charged with its day-to-day maintenance. In fact, in the same way that social mores have defined what is and what is not acceptable behaviour for a mother, it appears that Women's Studies is also required to conform to a similar code of propriety both of which rest upon the ideals of goodness, warmth, compassion, and benevolence. Just who is responsible for implementing this code, I cannot say. But I do know that it exists, for I have witnessed Women's Studies students being "pissed off" at a professor for not "understanding" and I have experienced it as a teaching assistant when I have felt compelled to both stay after class and receive telephone calls late into the night, listening to the personal problems of students.

Allow me to return at this point to my earlier use of the term "fraudulent," a word which I used to describe my feelings of alienation from and lack of allegiance to my programme. In some respects, it must seem rather silly to have such an attitude towards a course of study; indeed, would a physics student experience a similar form of estrangement from his/her science department? Perhaps they might, but I would tend to think not. Because in Women's Studies, unlike physics, students (as well as faculty) wittingly or unwittingly struggle with the impossible task of presenting only positive images of the programme so as to avoid exposing any of its weaknesses, since doing so is perceived as inviting negative repercussions onto a new and relatively vulnerable programme. Here, Gayatri Spivak's use of the term "crisis management"[20] is appropriate, for the consequences of this paradoxical — however well-intentioned — situation is that a "system" of ideas and/or behaviour becomes entrenched, wherein some ideas and perspectives are permitted and others prohibited — for the sake of preserving the system. In this way, subjectivity becomes easily ignored and/or erased and narrowly defined categories take over. This is ironic since part of the impetus of Women's Studies programmes came from the need to critique and deconstruct the very categories in which women were trapped.[21]

Although unrelenting in its tone, controversial theorist Camille Paglia's description of Women's Studies may hold some element of truth, for it touches upon the very problem of "crisis management" described above. She states:

> Women's Studies is a jumble of vulgarians, bunglers, whiners, French faddicts, apparatchiks, doughface party-liners, pie-in-the-sky utopianists, and bullying, sanctimonious sermon-

izers. Reasonable, moderate feminists hang back and, like good Germans, keep silent in the face of fascism.[22]

Paglia feels her remarks are not only justifiable, but necessary since Women's Studies programmes have made significant gains in terms of popularity and prestige, and have done so "virtually uncritiqued and unchecked."[23] When I first read this passage, I (guiltily) howled with laughter; rather than being offended, I was intrigued ... Women's Studies and fascism? Was it possible? Although I find the word "fascism" a bit extreme for this context and prefer her use of "party-line," I must admit that Paglia has provided me with an understanding of how it is that I came to regard myself as a traitor to my Women's Studies programme. The ideological promise/goal of sisterhood and what this entails lacked much in the way of any rigorous self-reflexive analysis, and it is in this way that the programme can be, itself, guilty of embracing categories in a dogmatic way. For example, the fact that Women's Studies has a tendency to blame all men and idealize all women ultimately contributed to my perception that I was being "anti-feminist" despite my genuine support of several of both Women's Studies' and the wider feminist movement's ideals.

Because there are many students and faculty alike of Women's Studies who "have trouble with the assumed fixed-ness and often ahistorical character of the categories feminists use to identify ... [themselves] and each other,"[24] what is to be done? Should the programme exist at all? Through its very existence in the educational institution, it is unavoidable that Women's Studies becomes, in some way, a part of the very process it critiques. Accepting this fact may require the giving up of its quest to be the "good mother," and handing over the responsibility of teaching feminist theory to the remaining university departments. Given the substantial increase in the number of programmes now in place, it is unlikely that such a transformation will take place anywhere in the near future. In fact, at this very moment Carleton University is gathering the necessary resources for a

Master's of Women's Studies programme. Whether female students are signing up for the scholarly training they will receive or whether it is for the fulfilment of some unmet emotional need, I am unable to say. What I can state, however, is that if Women's Studies were to expose some of its faults (which, by the way, traditional departments rarely do) or even close its doors, rather than such an occurrence being seen as a failure of community or "sisterhood," it will be condemned as a failure of (academic) feminism.[25] The backlash and resistance which the programme so desperately tries to avoid, will come crashing down with a vengeance complete with snide remarks and a "told-you-so" attitude.

In the end, the work which lies ahead of me in terms of my relationship to Women's Studies, and feminism in general, is acknowledging the fact that advocating women's liberation does not inevitably require allegiance to a homogeneous feminist value system, nor the avoidance of a critical self-reflexive stance. Because "women struggle and make feminist decisions, whether they call it that or not, in a million ways every single day,"[26] it is enough to define feminism in terms that are appropriate to individual circumstances and which satisfy individual needs and desires. Such a feminist politics necessarily consists of a solitary journey ... with the knowledge that there are other travellers out there like myself who are following their own country roads.

Notes

1. Bronwen Wallace, *Common Magic*, Oberon Press, (Canada: 1985).
2. The term "feminist movement" is, itself, a catachresis since there is no one single, identifiable group or organization of women working towards a commonly defined goal of women's equality. The use of this term throughout the chapter is, therefore, a rather ambiguous one; its meaning should be taken as that which is used within the realm of public discourse, the latter having more clearly defined social, economic, and political implications.

3. Himani Bannerji, et al. eds., *Unsettling Relations: the university as a site of feminist struggles,* Women's Press, (Toronto: 1991).

4. Punam Khosla, "From the Navel to the Fist: Feminists Working Against Tides of Individualism, Abstraction and Victimization." In *Resources For Feminist Research,* vol. 20, nos. 3 & 4, fall/winter 1991 "Transforming Knowledge and Politics," p. 98.

5. Kathleen Martindale, "What Is Known About Homophobia in the Classroom and the Limited Applicability of Anti-Homophobia Workshop Strategies for Women's Studies Classes." In *Canadian Woman Studies,* vol. 12, no. 3, spring 1992 "Gender Equity and Institutional Change," p. 95.

6. Christina Sommers, "Sister Soldiers." In *The New Republic,* October 5, 1992, issue #4,055, p. 30.

7. Gloria Bowles and Renate Duelli-Klein eds., *Theories of Women's Studies,* Routledge and Kegan Paul, (Boston: 1983).

8. Marguerite Andersen, "Empowerment Through Women's Studies." In *Resources For Feminist Research,* vol. 20, nos. 3 & 4, fall/winter 1991 "Transforming Knowledge and Politics," pp. 42-44.

9. Vivian P. Makosky and Michele A. Paludi, "Feminism and Women's Studies in the Academy." In *Foundations for a Feminist Restructuring of the Academic Disciplines,* eds. Michele Paludi and Gertrude A. Steuernagel, The Haworth Press, (New York: 1990), pp. 1-37.

10. Taly Rutenberg, "Learning Women's Studies." In *Theories of Women's Studies,* eds. Gloria Bowles and Renate Duelli-Klein, Routledge and Kegan Paul, (Boston: 1983), p. 77.

11. Joanne Prindiville and Cathryn Boak, "From the Straight Shore to the Labrador: Women's Studies as a Distance Education Course." In *Women's Education,* vol. 5, no. 4, summer 1987 "Learning At A Distance," p. 7.

12. Makosky and Paludi, "Feminism and Women's Studies in the Academy," p. 14.

13. Rosalind Coward, "Sexual Politics and Psychoanalysis: Some notes on their relation." In *Feminism, Culture and Politics,* eds. Rosalind Brunt and Caroline Rowan, Lawrence and Wishart, (London: 1982), p. 177.

14. op. cit., p. 178.

15. Susan Heald, "Pianos to Pedagogy: Pursuing the Educational Subject." In *Unsettling Relations: the university as a site of feminist struggles,* eds. Himani Bannerji, et al., Women's Press, (Toronto: 1991), p. 135.

16. Dorothy Smith, *The Everyday World As Problematic: A Feminist Sociology,* Northeastern University Press, (Boston: 1987), p. 7.

17. Patricia Eliot, *From Mastery to Analysis: Theories of Gender in Psychoanalytic Feminism,* Cornell University Press, (Ithaca, NY: 1991), p. 23.

18. Prindiville and Boak, "From the Straight Shore to the Labrador: Women's Studies as a Distance Education Course," p. 7.

19. Sarah Brooke, student in the "Introduction to Women's Studies" course of 1992/93.

20. Gayatri Chakravorty Spivak, as quoted in *The Post-Colonial Critic: Interviews, Strategies, Dialogues,* ed., Sarah Harasym, Routledge, (New York: 1990), pp. 95-112.

21.   This idea was one of many insightful remarks given to me by Donna Jowett in the grading of a term paper, and for this I owe her much thanks.

22.   Camille Paglia, *Sex, Art, and American Culture,* Vintage Books, (New York: 1992), p. 244.

23.   *Ibid.,* p. 262.

24.   Kari Dehli, "Leaving the Comfort of Home: Working through Feminisms." In *Unsettling Relations: the university as a site of feminist struggles,* eds. Himani Bannerji, et al., Women's Press, (Toronto: 1991), p. 46.

25.   Wendy Kaminer, "Feminism's Identity Crisis." In *The Atlantic Monthly,* vol. 272, no. 4, October 1993, p. 66.

26.   Naomi Wolf, as quoted in "Get Real About Feminism — The Myths, the Backlash, the Movement." In *Ms.,* vol. 4, no. 2, September/October 1993, p. 42.

6

The Space-Between Ethics and Politics:
Or, More of the Same?

Geraldine Finn

This chapter was originally written as a keynote presentation for the Annual Meeting of the Canadian Society for the Study of Practical Ethics which was held at Queen's University in Kingston, Ontario in May 1991. The subject of the conference was Feminist Approaches to Practical Ethics, and I was asked to address this question in my opening remarks. I used the opportunity to continue a reflection on the relationship between ethics and politics with which I had been engaged for some time.[1] So, although the question of *feminist* ethics provided the occasion for this particular presentation, and a concrete and immediate example of the issues involved in thinking ethics and politics together, the problematic it addresses extends beyond feminism (or any other particular politics) to the *question of ethics* itself — the question which *is* ethics, as I argue below — and its relationship to the political exigencies of our language(s) and lives.

I argue here that ethics (ethical experience, knowledge, value, truth, reality) is precisely that which puts politics into question from the standpoint of *the space-between*: the space between category and reality, the space of the ethical encounter with the other as other and not more of the Same. That an ethics which relies on the (political) categories of established thought and/or seeks to solidify or cement them — into institutionalized rights and freedoms, rules and regulations, and principles of practice, for example — is not so much an ethics, therefore, *as an abdication of ethics for politics* under another description. As it exchanges the undecidability, the an-archy, the responsibility of the space-between of the ethical encounter with others for the security, the hier-archy, of the pre-scribed and pre-scriptive places of the categories. Ethical praxis cannot *renounce* politics because it is actually constituted by it, in the space between experience and the (political) categories which organize its *sens*. But it cannot simply identify with politics either for then it would lose its specificity as ethical — as that which brings the political into view as *politics*, i.e. as an effect and strategy of the organization of power (rather than nature, or choice) and as an appropriate object therefore for judgment, contestation, intervention, and change.

Community is absent from this text. This is not an accidental but a constitutive and strategic absence. For the absence of community in *the space-between* (category and reality, language(s) and lives) is present(ed) in the text as the very condition (of possibility) of ethics. While the abandonment of ethics to politics in the name of its presence (in the name of community) is its insistent theme. To make this relationship between ethics and politics and (the absence/presence of) community more explicit an occasional (community) has been inserted into this text from which it was originally absent to mark the place of its absence and the trace(s) of its presenting.

* * *

For the past several years I have been trying to understand the relationship between ethics and politics: between ethical realities, convictions, experiences, principles, purposes and ends and political realities, convictions, experiences, principles, purposes and ends. And I am happy to report that I have recently come to some conclusions which I will be sharing with you today.

My point of departure in this reflection has been that ethics and politics are *not* the same and that attempts to reduce one to the other, while tempting and comforting and in some sense enabling — whichever way the reduction operates: ethics to politics or vice versa

— never do justice to the complexity and particularity of the concrete issues involved. I now think that these reductive moves, to collapse ethics and politics into each other, also sabotage the ethical and/or political motivations and ends they are usually intended to serve. Nevertheless, it seems to me that this is in fact the direction most efforts take when thinking and practicing ethics and politics together: resolving into some form or other of either a classical "idealist" position which privileges ethics, and posits politics as merely ethics writ large (characteristic of but not exclusive to the political Right), or, the alternative "materialist" position which privileges politics and posits ethics as merely politics writ small (characteristic of but not exclusive to the political Left). What I have been trying to develop is an understanding and practice of ethics and politics *together* which preserves the specificity of each while honoring their inherent and inevitable connectedness.

I believe everyone has an ethics, just as everyone has a politics, whether or not they articulate, acknowledge, or deny it. What I mean by this is that our choices and actions are always to some extent grounded in and motivated by our experiences and assumptions about the nature, value and meaning of human existence in general and our own lives in particular. And this is what I mean by "having an ethics." Likewise, our choices and actions are always in some sense and to some extent grounded in and motivated by our experiences and assumptions about the nature, value and meaning of power in general and our own relationship to it in particular. And this is what I mean by "having a politics."

These two sets of experiences, knowledges and realities — the ethical and the political — are obviously connected. Ethical experience (knowledge and reality) always and only occurs within the context of power, i.e. within a social situation already organized and interpreted by and for specific political interests, agents and ends. While politics, the social organization and institutionalisation of power, only and always occurs within the context of an ethics which can enable and excuse it. The subtleties and specifics of this relation-ship between ethical and political realities (experiences, knowledges, values and ends) and the implications of this for (feminist) praxis are the subject of this paper.

Since ethical praxis always occurs within a particular political context (community), it will (either by default or design) *confirm* the values, goals and ends of the political situation within which it is situated and thereby the hierarchies of power and control which they enable and sustain, *or* it will contest them. Ethical praxis, that is, will either *endorse* a particular society's vision of the "good life," the life worth living and dying for which is discursively and concretely em-bodied in its landscape, architecture and institutions as much as it is in its actual ideologies; or it will call that vision and those institutions into question. I espouse the kind of ethical praxis which puts the values, principles and practices of the political status quo and the vision of the "good life" which animates and is animated by it into question. In fact, I go further than this to define ethical praxis in these terms: *in terms of* the question which *is* ethics, an ethics which must al-ways pose the question *of* ethics, and put the political status quo into question.

Ethical praxis which merely rearticulates the values and goals of the status quo to realities identified as problematic for it, seems to me to consist not so much in *ethical* interventions directed towards fun-damental issues of right and wrong and the constitution of the good life, as *technical* — and for that reason, *political* — interventions directed towards the fine tuning of the norms and procedures already in place to accommodate new realities within the system which might otherwise disturb its hierarchies of power and control or its ap-pearance of Reason and Right. Thus, much of what passes for "ethi-cal" in the theories and practices of professional, practical and applied ethics is not really ethical at all from this point of view, but technical-political in the given sense. For they do not actually raise or address *ethical* questions about the implicit or explicit values animating and directing the arguments, institutions and practices under their scrutiny and the society which has produced them; but rather technical, pragmatic, logistical, *political* questions about professional etiquette, accountability and control, and the policing of the boundaries of competing individual and institutional jurisdictions.

Calls for the construction of an alternative feminist ethics,[2] or for a code of ethics for feminist praxis — in business, medicine, or research, for example, — tend to fall under this description: raising not so much *ethical* questions about the fundamental norms and values animating Western society and its institutionalized practices and priorities; nor even *ethical* questions about the values animating feminism in general or its own feminist agenda in particular; but *technical-political* questions about extending or modifying the norms and values already in place to accommodate women and/or feminist criticisms or practices which have been done in their name. They are, that is, more about regulation, accountability and control, than ethics.

This tendency to pre-empt the ethical question(s) by and for technical-political ones, characterises most feminist praxis, including that which explicitly calls itself ethical. This includes feminist interventions in sexuality and reproduction, for example (around issues of abortion, pornography, sexual preference, custody, new reproductive technologies, etc.); in economics (on issues of affirmative action, equal pay for work of equal value, pensions, housework, welfare ... and so on); in the areas of physical and mental health (around questions of consent, and the medicalisation of women's bodies); and in the various movements for peace and protection of the environment. Feminist interventions in these and other areas — both practical and theoretical — tend not to *challenge* the *ethical* premises of the institutions and practices which are the focus of their concern, but rather to *use* them to criticise the political praxis which is done in their name. They do not pose the ethical question (the question which *is* ethics, the question *of* ethics) but, on the contrary, assume the ethical premises of the system as adequate to and for their own struggles against it.

Feminist praxis tends, that is, to pre-empt ethical enquiry and thus the possibility of forging the conditions for real change — for the fulfilment of its own radical ends — by articulating its criticisms and objectives in terms of the categories and values already endorsed by and institutionalized in the political realities we are struggling to change: the values of autonomy, control, freedom, equality, identity, ownership, choice, utility, agency, reason, responsibility, and rights. These are the authorised and regulatory categories of moral debate in our society. So much so, that if you do not express yourself in their terms you will not be heard as having an ethics worthy of the name nor, therefore, an argument or cause worthy of discussion, respect or public debate. Claims to moral goods which are not or cannot be articulated within these authorised categories of Western thought are ruled out of court: out of the discursive domains of both ethics and politics as irrelevant, idiosyncratic, arbitrary, atavistic, subjective, sentimental, naive, or merely "relative"; as gratuitous personal or culturally specific whims beyond rational accountability or, therefore, collective intervention or control; as matters of aesthetics — of taste and "lifestyle" — rather than ethics; matters for individual and personal and not collective and political agency, responsibility or change.

It is entirely understandable then that feminists should make their claims against the system in terms the system recognises as reasonable, rational, and possibly right. Indeed, it is more than understandable, it is absolutely indispensable to feminist praxis as it is to any and all politics. But it is not enough, and it is certainly not *ethical* in the sense proposed here, if this is *all* we do. We must at the same time question the values we are obliged to invoke in making our claims against the political status quo: the values of freedom, identity, equality, choice and control, for example; the values of liberal individualism upon which the contemporary *polis* relies for its legitimation, reproduction and control. We may have to articulate our claims against that *polis* in its terms, but we do not have to *believe* in them. Indeed, we must not believe in them, for they actually betray the truth of our political praxis: its ethical motivation, and its condition of possibility in the space-between the categories of political thought. This I will now explain.

There would not be dissent, disaffection, resistance, or change (or social or individual pathology, for that matter) if the articulated and authoritative categories, norms and values of society were adequate to experience; in other words, if language were commensurate with life, or representation with reality. But this is not the case. The contingent and changing concrete world always exceeds the ideal categories of thought within which we attempt to express and contain it. And the same is true of people. We are always both more and less than the categories which name and divide us. More and less, that is, than a woman, a man, a Christian, a Jew, a mother, a worker, a wife. More and less than *what we stand for in the polis and what stands for us.* Our lives leave remainders (they say more than they mean) just as our categories leave residues (they mean more than they say). Lives and categories are incommensurable. They exceed each other, leaving in their wake a fertile precipitate of an-archical *sens* or *signifiance*[3] which ex-sists beyond and between given categorical frameworks — beyond and between the knowable and the already known — as an always available (re)source of difference, resistance, and change: of being-otherwise-than-being a re-presentation of an already instituted (and therefore *pre*-scribed, *pre*-dicated, and *pre*-determined) (community) category or class: man, woman, child, Christian, Muslim, Jew.

This space between category and experience, representation and reality, language and life, is, I believe, the necessary and indispensable space of judgement; of creativity and value, resistance and change. It is the ground of the critical intentions and originating experiences which enable us to call the status quo into question and challenge the already known universe and its organisation into the predicative and prescriptive categories of practical reason. It constitutes the space and the experience within which the conventionality, the contingency, the arbitrariness, of the familiar realities of the natural attitude — of its categorical positivities and identities — can be seen and challenged.

In another context I identified this space as the space and ground of "spirituality" and "desire"[4] i.e. of our experience of and aspiration to "transcendence": not of the *flesh* of the material world itself, but of the categories which frame and contain it and the possibilities of our own being within it. It is as such *the* ethical space, the space of the specifically *ethical* encounter with others (with otherness) as *other* and not more of the same: as otherwise-than-being simply a re-presenta-tion of a pre-conceived, pre-scribed, pre-determined and thus pre-dicative category and class — a re-presentation which relieves us of the ethical responsibility of attending to the particularity of the other and inventing our relationship with it (him or her). By contrast, the space-between reality and representation presents me with, puts me in the presence of, that which has never been there before: the other in all its singularity as a visitation, an epiphany (to use Levinas' terms)[5], an absolute exteriority which cannot without violence be in-tegrated into the Same. It is a presenting, a presence which puts *me* into question as well as the relationship, the world, and the common sense *(sens commun)* we may or may not share. It is an encounter which demands/commands me to think and be anew: to risk being-otherwise-than-being what I have already become.

Managing this silent but nevertheless signifying *(signifiant)* space between the pre-thematic an-archical/ethical and the categorical/hier-archical encounter with others — this space of the otherwise-than-being a re-presentation of a pre-existing category or class — is absolutely central to the exercise of political power and to the or-ganisation of our subjection to it; absolutely central, that is, to our "subjectivity": our being as subjects of experiences and actions which "count" (or don't count as the case may be): of sentences which make sense (sens) in the *polis:* central to our access to language and thus to our social status and survival. (Which should give us pause, therefore, when claiming our "identities" as women, blacks, gays or lesbians for example: as anything other than a provisional strategic political claim for provisional, strategic political ends. I will be coming back to this later). Categorical schemas and institutionalised discourses (the discourses of politics, ethics, philosophy, science, religion, spirituality, sport, sex, literature and art, for example) work towards this end of managing and, in our own society, suturing — though this need not be the case — this vital ethical space between representation and reality, language and life.[6] They channel the affective anarchical ethical residues and remainders of experience (of being-otherwise-than-being) into authorised categorical hierarchical meanings, intentionalities, and desires compatible with and amenable to the controlling interests of prevailing political powers.

All political praxis speaks to and from this space, this irrepressible precipitate of being and thought, this constant (re)source of differance,[7] disruption and change. *Conservative* politics speaks to it in order to contain, deny or negate its excesses: to recuperate its deviations and differance into and for the hegemonic categories and relations which constitute and sustain the status quo. Radical or revolutionary politics, like feminism, speaks to and from the same precipitate (the same space between representation and reality) to *affirm* it: to inhabit and extend it and to organize it against the status quo for political resistance and change. At least radical politics must begin here, as any critical moment must, in the *experience of disjuncture*, of the incommensurability between language and life, between authorised categories of experience and experience itself. Radical politics must originate here in the as-yet untamed excesses and precipitates (residues and remainders) of language and lives, and take its inspiration and direction — at least in the beginning — from the anarchical ethical relation with others which occurs there between and beyond the categorical imperatives of regulated institutionalised thought. But it cannot remain here if it is to become practical in politics, for to do that it must subordinate its original/originating *ethical* motivations and ends to the strategic necessities of political action within and against the *polis* on its terms — the only terms it will recognise as rational and real.

What concerns me is not that this *subordination of ethics* to *politics* takes place. On the contrary, I recognise it to be an indispensable and inevitable moment of political practice: of engaging in politics for the purpose of producing change. What concerns me is that this truth of the ethical encounter with others/with otherness and its strategic sub-ordination to the exigencies of politics is obfuscated by politics itself: neither recognised, nor acknowledged, nor therefore managed or mourned by or within the theories and practices of the would-be radi-cal and resisting politics (communities) it actually inspires. And this means that the ethical motivations of politics, in the space between and beyond the categories of the political itself, are lost to its own self-consciousness and, more seriously, abandoned in its praxis. Just as they have been lost and abandoned in the theories and practices of the conservative politics to which they are opposed. And this is what concerns me.

We see this lapse, this collapse, of ethics into politics — this aban-donment of liberation for regulation and repression — repeatedly in the trajectories of political movements which begin as movements of resis-tance or reform. I do not think we need to despair or become cynical about this, as conservative political theorists might suggest, attributing it to the inexorable logic of power, for example, or an inherent failure of human nature. We should rather seek to situate it within the exigencies and antinomies of politics itself and the complexities of the relationship between ethical and political truth. For this disappearance of the ethical into the political, in politics which begin as movements of liberation grounded in the ethical encounter with others/with otherness, while alarming, is not surprising. We live in a society which systematically deprives us of a language and a context within which this experience of the space between category and reality can be acknowledged, in-habited, or even named — except as pathological:[8] something to be fixed up or abandoned; a society which actually obfuscates — denies, distorts and mystifies — the possibilities and realities of ethical experience, of the ethical encounter with others as other (and not more of the same) — the only encounter which makes a difference and demands a responsibility from me which is not already *pre*-scribed. I do not believe that this is an accidental effect of the discursive and institutional organization of power in Western society but rather, on the contrary, a systematic strategy which keeps us tied to our political identities, our tribes (as man, woman, child, black, white, Christian, Jew, etc.); tied to categories that divide and contain us and organise our respective places in the *polis*; which individualise us as appropriate, accessible and amenable surfaces/subjects for the applications and manipulations of power; and which thereby supply us with our particular interests and *stakes* in the status quo.

It saddens me, nevertheless to see the same abandonment of ethics to politics in the theories and practices of contemporary politics (communities) of resistance and change, like feminism, in their tendency to assume the terms and relevancies of the politics they purport to reject in the articulation of their own values and ends: the categories of self and other, identity and difference, man and woman, freedom and necessity, for example. As if these categories of thought were commensurate with the contingent and concrete realities they organize and describe; and as if the categories, the realities, and the relationship between them were unambivalent and transparent. It is as if we are afraid to "come out" from the categories which, uncomfortable and contradictory as the lives they afford us may be, at least supply us with a place in the *polis* and with the mask of re-presentation and authority; with a voice that can be heard *as and because* it is re-presentative of an identifiable category or class, an identifiable political subject and interest: the identity, subjectivity, and interest of black, native, lesbian, white, or working women, for example.

Organising under and identifying with the category which articulates our inclusions and exclusions in and from the *polis* (with the

category of woman, lesbian, black, native ... and so on) may be necessary for winning for ourselves (as women, lesbians, blacks, native
women) more and better space within it. But if this is as far as our
political gesture goes — if it stops with the already instituted
categories themselves — then it is not really subversive of the politics
with which it is engaged nor, and this I think is more important, of the
ethics upon which that politics depends and which it in turn
reproduces in its praxis.[9]

Our lives exceed the categories that organize our relationship to
power and to each other. And it is this experience of excess which is
the condition of possibility of resistance and dissent in the first place.
Claiming that excess against the category which names and contains
us broadens the political scope of the category and thus the political
scope of our lives. It is, in this sense, liberating. But it leaves the
category and the political system it articulates intact and available for
recuperation and control by, for, and within the ruling apparatus —
even if it includes new personnel — if this is all it does. If it does not at
the same time continue to pose the ethical question — the question of
ethics, the question which is ethics — the question of our *ethical* relations with others. And this means questioning the politics and practices of (political) *re-presentation* itself: the organization of experience
and affect into discrete and exclusive categories of being (of identity)
through which our encounter with the world and others is mediated
as always already pre-dicative and pre-scriptive and, thus, un-
response-able to the otherness of others and the possibilities of difference and change.

If politics is only politics — getting the best deal possible, seeking,
keeping and exercising power — i.e. if politics fails to acknowledge or
inhabit or nurture the space-between of our ethical relations with
others/with otherness, then no matter how radical or subversive its
claims and self-conscious ends, it will always end up reproducing the
instrumentalities and ends of its point of departure, of the regime it
purports to oppose. It is disturbing to see contemporary politics of

identity in some of its most accessible and increasingly institutionalised manifestations doing just that: taking familiar political
representations of reality at face-value (the representations of liberal
individualism: the categories of rights and freedoms, self and other,
identity and difference) and rejecting or reforming them as the case
may be. Speaking not from the *space-between* reality and representation, between context and text, which permits the political critique in the first place; but *from the places prescribed by the ruling
representations themselves*: the spaces of the modernist (liberal-
democratic) text — of the abstract, disembodied subject of freedom
and rights. The politics of identity risks binding us thereby all the
more securely and narrowly to and within the politics it is actually
struggling against: to and within the re-presentations and categories,
the identities and values, of the political status quo: the sedimented
meanings, instrumentalities and ends of liberalism, and the increasingly atomised, volatilised, fragmented, divided, divisive, and
impoverished categories of subjective/subjected being upon which the
contemporary version of its project depends.

A specifically *ethical* political praxis would consist in resisting this
movement of institutionalisation: this inherent tendency of contemporary politics to obfuscate and abandon its ethical conditions of possibility in the experience of the space-between, in the interest of
making claims and consolidating political gains. A specifically ethical
political praxis would consist in honoring and nurturing, acknowledging, inhabiting, and *speaking from* the space-between representation and reality, language and life, category and experience: the
space of the ethical encounter with others as other and not more of
the same; a space and an encounter which puts *me* into question,
which challenges and changes me, as well as the other (the otherness
of the other) and the socius/the system (community) which contains
and sustains us. It is a praxis which will cost me something if it is effective. A praxis of the absolutely particular[10] for which there can be
no rules, no codes, no principles and no guarantees. A praxis of risk

and response-ability in which, I believe, lies our only hope for real political change.

Notes

1. See "The Politics of Contingency: The Contingency of Politics: On the Political Implications of Merleau-Ponty's Ontology of the Flesh," in Thomas Busch and Shawn Gallagher, eds., *Merleau-Ponty, Hermeneutics, and Postmodernism* (New York: SUNY, 1992); and "The Politics of Spirituality: The Spirituality of Politics" in Phillipa Berry and Andrew Wernick, eds., *Shadow of Spirit: Postmodernism and Religion* (London: Routledge, 1992), (also in *Listening. Journal of Religion and Culture*, Vol.27, No.2, Spring 1992). See also *Why Althusser Killed His Wife. Essays on Discourse and Violence* (forthcoming from Humanities Press, 1994).

2. As in the following, for example: Carol Gilligan, *In a Different Voice* (Cambridge: Harvard University Press, 1982); Nel Noddings, *Caring* (Berkeley: University of California Press, 1984); Sara Ruddick, *Maternal Thinking. Toward a Politics of Peace* (Boston: Beacon Press, 1989); Lorraine Code, Sheila Mullett and Christine Overall, eds., *Feminist Perspectives: Philosophical Essays on Method and Morals* (Toronto: Toronto University Press, 1988); Marwenna Griffiths and Margaret Whitford, eds., *Feminist Perspectives in Philosophy* (Bloomington: Indiana University Press, 1988).

3. *Sens* in French means both direction (or way) and meaning; *signifiance* (from the verb *signifier*: to signify, mean) refers to signifying as an *activity* (to be distinguished from *signification*: significance, meaning; which refers to the object of activity, or to an already accomplished or given meaning).

4. "The Politics of Spirituality: The Spirituality of Politics" (op. cit.)

5. See, for example, Emmanuel Levinas, *Collected Philosophical Papers*, translated by Alphonso Lingis (The Hague: Martinus Nijhoff, 1987).

6. "The Politics of Spirituality: The Spirituality of Politics" (op. cit.) describes how the discourse(s) of spirituality and religion manage/suture the space-between of this ethical encounter with others.

7. "Differance is what makes the movement of signification possible only if each element that is said to be 'present', appearing on the stage of presence, is related to something other than itself but retains the mark of a past element and already lets itself be hollowed out by the mark of its relation to a future element. This trace relates no less to what is called the future than to what is called the past, and it constitutes what is called the present by this very relation to what it is not, to what it absolutely is not;" (Jacques Derrida, "Differance" in *Speech and Phenomena And Other Essays on Husserl's Theory of Signs*, translated by David Allison, Evanston: Northwestern University Press, 1973, p.142-143). Derrida's neologism *differance* refers to the activity of differing/deferring which is constitutive of sense/*sens*: to the movement of (the production of) differences

without origin or end which makes meaning both possible and ultimately and always undecidable. In my terms, it designates the incommensurability of language and life: the (ethical) space between category and experience.

8. As, for example, in the discourses and practices of sociology, psychology, psychiatry, criminology, sexology, pedagogy, etc.

9. An ethics of freedom and rights which is founded on liberal notions of the self — as discrete, identifiable, proprietorial, and singular with discrete, identifiable, proprietorial, and singular interests, origins and ends. An ethics which thereby denies the reality of the space-between and, thus, the reality of the ethical encounter with others it makes possible; and correspondingly, therefore, the possibility of a different political ethic — an ethic of differance — such as the one proposed here.

10. Particularity is not the same as individuality: it does not imply the exclusivity of an I-dentity for which others are other, as individuality does; nor, correspondingly, the inclusivity of a self who is sufficient ("present" in Derrida's sense — see note 7 above) to itself. Particularity, contingency, and the flesh are key terms in my efforts to elaborate a specifically *ethical* political practice. See, for example, "The Politics of Contingency: The Contingency of Politics" (op. cit.); "Why Are There No Great Women Postmodernists?" in Valda Blundell, John Shepherd and Ian Taylor, eds., *Relocating Cultural Studies. Developments in Theory and Research* (London: Routledge, 1993); and "The Politics of Postmodernism: Postmodernism as Ideology and Effect," and other essays, in *Why Althusser Killed His Wife*, op. cit.

7

When the System Farms the Farmers: What Can We Do About the Saskatchewan Farm Crisis?

Christopher Lind

I may not know as much about the world market as some of those professionals out there, but what I do know is that it's wrong. It's all wrong and we've got to change it.

I've seen farmers who've died. They did all the spraying. I've never had a doctor tell me but the women of the community knew how he died — chemicals, kidney failure and all that.

This essay forms one part of a larger study of the moral economy[1] of the farm crisis in Saskatchewan. The study has proceeded on the basis of interviews with farmers involved in farm protest. All of the interviews have been conducted with people involved in the Rosetown Rally, a farm rally that took place in October of 1991 in Rosetown, Saskatchewan. Many of the farmers interviewed helped to organize the rally and have gone on to organize other rallies and a loose organization known as the Concerned Farmers of Saskatchewan.[2] I have used the interviews not only to generate data on the moral categories used by farmers but also as a guide to the issues bound up in the many crises that together, form what is generally known as the farm crisis in Saskatchewan.

In the course of my interviews, a number of themes have emerged. They include the significance of agriculture to national sovereignty, the simultaneous erosion of and need for co-operation and community, the shifting of the crisis from the farm operation to the farm family and the unfairness of the international trading system. Included among these themes are concerns about powerlessness and a related perception that the farm community is no longer in charge of its own destiny — that it is the farmers who are now being farmed. Later on in the interviews, after some trust has been established, concerns are also expressed about the effect of current agricultural practice on the environment. It is this last concern that this essay will address in the context of an overriding sense of powerlessness and loss of community.

Powerlessness

The farmers involved in farm protest are clearly frustrated by their own seeming inability to affect their fortunes. For some years in the 1980s, many people took the approach that the hard times were part of a cyclical winnowing process that goes on in all industries. Certainly some younger farmers were losing their land, but many people took this as an indication of poor management ability or poor timing. The late 1980s saw several years of drought and an infestation of grasshoppers. Many experienced farmers said that all they needed were one or two good years and things would be all right again. In terms of production, the 1990 and 1991 crop years saw the second and third largest yields on record in Saskatchewan. It was after these two "good years" that many people realized they were worse off than before. When the cost of production ranges from \$5-\$7/bushel, the farmers respond that "we are forced to accept \$2/bushel for the best damn wheat in the world."

While people are divided on what exactly is the "real cause," clearly the trade war between Europe and the United States is one factor. The moral analysis of the farmers is that "what these countries are doing to us is internationally immoral and an abomination on world trade." From their point of view, current practice is contrary to elementary notions of fair trade. "Stop this debilitating madness," they shout, "and start trading fairly." The widespread sense of powerlessness is internalized in the farm community. They want and expect to be able to solve their own problems but are unable to. "We feel the blame that others seem to be putting on us."

The powerlessness of farmers as a group is brought home painfully when individual farmers face foreclosure by banks and other financial institutions. In these cases, farmers feel abandoned by the institutions that encouraged the debt in the first place. "What protection does the farmer have? What protection does the bank have?" In many rural municipalities more than 30% of the farmers have appeared before either federal or provincial farm debt review agencies. Nothing evokes the theme of powerlessness better than the image of slavery and slave labour. These metaphors come easily to hand for people who work harder and harder and see fewer and fewer results. "Farm labour is slave labour." "Fifty percent of the farm population is farmer's wives. Our labour is slave labour." "We can no longer work like slaves and work more and more for less and less."

It is this widespread feeling of powerlessness that causes members of the farm community to think of themselves as objects of agricultural practice rather than as subjects, though that is not exactly the language used to express it. They would express it this way. "The governments and societies of North America decided years ago that food is a given and the farming population is taken for granted. Whatever it takes to keep them producing out there ... do it." "Food is the last thing that anybody thinks about ... It's like the sun coming up every day." "The farmer and his wife are now expected to work off the farm to support the farming habit." "The system is farming the farmers."

Loss of Community

Another key moral theme expressed by the interviewees had to do with the loss and absence of community. Farm people were concerned about the eroding base of their communities. They recognized that they had failed to work together in the past and they called on each other to show the level of co-operation that would be required to survive. "We need to get together or we'll all be gone," they said to one another. "By ourselves we are all dust." They acknowledged that there were forces that were driving them apart and that private (self) interest had triumphed in the past. "We need to work together and co-operate for the common good." This claim was widely applauded at the Rosetown Rally. "We can have an impact because we came here together today," they said.

A strong connection was also being made between the sustainability of farm families and the sustainability of rural communities. "Tell the people that they're going to have to start supporting the family farm. Make sure you put *family* farm in there. We don't want corporate farms. Co-ops are okay but we don't want huge corporations in here. Let the families stay out there. We want the community to stay there." The theme of community was obviously connected in an intimate way with the crisis facing farm families. There was a crisis in the institution of the family farm that metastasized into a crisis in the community of the family.

Concern for the Environment

One of the themes that emerged frequently in my interviews was a concern for the prairie soils and the prairie environment. Interestingly, the concern emerged only late in each of the conversations. Most farmers thought that the farmers themselves had the greatest self-interest at stake in environmentally sound farming practices ("Who has a greater concern for health than me? I'm the one who has to handle the stuff." "Most of us are Greenpeacers at heart") though at least one thought that government support programmes should be tied to maintaining a minimum level of fertility in the soil. The concern over declining fertility is a response to actual practice. As one farmer put it, "I try to be conservative in a lot ways. Not only for economic reasons, but to preserve this land. It has only been farmed for eighty-five years, maybe eighty years, and I'm sure that it has deteriorated and lost half of its original nutrients. I am trying not to make it any worse than that." Others indicate that the farmers alone can't do it.

The most frequently heard explanation was that economic conditions were working against good practice. One farmer said "Farmers need to be able to afford conservation." Another suggested that "you won't get any movement to proper land husbandry until you get something that will give you some decent return." Still another described it in terms of his own story. "When we broke this land up 100 years ago, there was 450 lbs. of available nitrogen to feed plants. Do you know what's left now? I've got land with 10 lbs. I've got good land with around 50 or 60 lbs. of available nitrogen left. We have sold 400 lbs. of nitrogen in that wonderful resource called prairie land. We've sold it over the last 100 years for nothing. Now what happens? Now you've got to put that nitrogen back in and $2 wheat won't buy any nitrogen. Somebody's going to have to pay for this or it won't grow … [We're] mining the land."

Environmentally-sound farming practice was not only linked to stable economics it was also linked to stable communities. In the context of a conversation on environmental issues, one farmer indicated that "we need to be able to maintain rural communities at a minimum acceptable level." Another suggested that "there's no better incentive for good husbandry than knowing your grandchildren will inherit the land."

Our problem is as follows: the farmers involved in farm protest are describing a moral economy of powerlessness where they feel blamed for problems they want to solve but cannot. Among the problems that need solving is the continuing degradation of the environment, yet they are being denied the economic and social stability that seems to be required. Is it possible to interpret these concerns in a more systematic way and in a way that reveals positive, possible alternatives?

The Farm Crisis is an Environmental Crisis

The farm crisis is not a single crisis. The many separate crises combine to form a common, collective social crisis, one that is destroying rural Saskatchewan. Among the many crises contributing to this result is the crisis in the prairie environment, one with several distinguishing features. These include soil erosion by the action of wind and water, loss of soil fertility, soil salinization, soil acidification, loss of genetic diversity, and the destruction of wildlife.

In 1984, the Canadian Senate, through its Standing Committee on Agriculture, Fisheries and Forestry, produced a report on the declining quality of Canadian soils. In that report, the committee concluded that "Canada risks permanently losing a large portion of its agricultural capacity if a major commitment to conserving the soil is not made immediately by all levels of government and by all Canadians."[3] Though the Senate report is referred to from time to time, no significant action has been taken to change the situation.

In 1992 the United Nations published a report indicating that in North America 95.5 million hectares of soil have been degraded by human activity since the end of World War II. Soil degradation is defined as "human-induced phenomena which lowers the current and/or future capacity of the soil to support human life." The degree of degradation can vary from light to extreme. Light degradation can be reversed by on-farm practices such as crop rotation and minimum tillage. Moderate degradation requires more resources than the average farm can provide, such as a national programme with financial incentives and technical help. Severely eroded land requires restoration beyond the ability of most developing nations. Extreme degradation means restoration is impossible. 10.6% of all vegetated land in North America has been degraded to varying degrees since 1945.[4]

Soil degradation has many causes. One of the causes is wind erosion. Saskatchewan is know for its big blue sky and its persistent, strong wind. When soil is left uncovered, that is, unplanted or otherwise exposed to the elements, the prairie wind picks up the nutrient rich topsoil and deposits it in gullies or streams or in the next province — places where it will no longer be used to nurture crops. Conventional methods of grain farming make the land extremely vulnerable to wind erosion.

When the land was ploughed for the first time at the turn of the century, new agricultural practices were introduced to manage the dry prairie soils. A common practice was summerfallowing. [5] This practice was a way of conserving moisture in a dry climate and saving nutrients for the next crop year. "The total land now subject to summerfallow each year makes up 13%, 24% and 38% of the cultivated land in Manitoba, Alberta and Saskatchewan, respectively."[6] In some regions of both Saskatchewan and Alberta it tops 40%.[7] This practice has had two long-term negative consequences. The first consequence is a loss of fertility due to the loss of top soil. Though it is difficult to accurately measure the extent of soil erosion, "it is estimated that the annual soil loss on the Prairies by wind is about ... 160 million tonnes."[8] Leaving fields covered with the stubble of the previous years crops, or trash, reduces the maximum possible soil erosion by 60%.[9]

A second consequence is the loss of organic matter which helps to bind the soil and retain the nutrients. Soil with less organic matter blows away more easily. Depleted soil is also more vulnerable to erosion by water. "It has been estimated that some 30% of cropland in the Prairie Provinces is exposed to potentially serious productivity losses from water erosion."[10]

The loss of soil fertility is not sudden but gradual and "while prairie soils are naturally high in organic matter content, they have lost nearly 45% of their original content since cultivation began there at the turn of the century."[11] But wind erosion is not the only factor leading to fertility loss.

The tilling of field in preparation for leaving it fallow has resulted in the release of much more nitrogen than is used by the next crop. A recent report prepared for the Royal Society of Canada suggests that two-thirds of the nitrogen released in this way and at least some of the phosphorous, are not used by the crops.[12] This loss of natural fertility has been masked by the use of imported fertility, in particular nitrogen fertilizer.

The amount of fertilizer used in Canadian agriculture is significant and increasing. From 1979 to 1989 Canadian farmers expanded their fertilizer use from 38 kilos per hectare to 47 kilos per hectare, an increase of 24%.[13] If we look at a smaller example over a larger period of time, however, the increase is dramatic. In Saskatchewan between 1971 and 1989 the amount of fertilizer used rose by over six times (see figure 1). This increase masks the degradation because agricultural production has risen even as the soil fertility has declined. For example, between 1980 and 1990, cereal production in Canada increased by 19%.[14] But expanded fertilizer use also contributes to environmental degradation. It decreases naturally occurring fertility and increases soil acidification.

As the entymologist Stuart Hill put it, "the application of highly soluble nitrogen fertilizers to soil inhibits free living and symbiotic nitrogen-fixing organisms. The growth of the vegetation then becomes dependent on these artificial inputs."[15] This means that where nitrogen fertilizer had been added to enhance fertility, it can have the opposite effect of depressing the activity of existing organisms essential for the production of naturally occurring nitrogen.

The increasing acidity of soils can be caused by the chemical reactions that result from the heavy use of nitrogen fertilizers although it can also be caused by the application of sulphur and by acid rain. It is counteracted by the application of lime. Though it is a greater problem in eastern Canada, in western Canada it is estimated that "a minimum of ... 350,000 tonnes of lime per year are needed just to maintain the present pH levels of the most affected soils."[16]

Increasing soil salinity is considered by some to be the major soil degradation problem in the Prairie Provinces. Here too, the practice of summerfallow is implicated. Summerfallow reduces the organic con-

Figure 1

Increase in Chemical use on Saskatchewan Farms

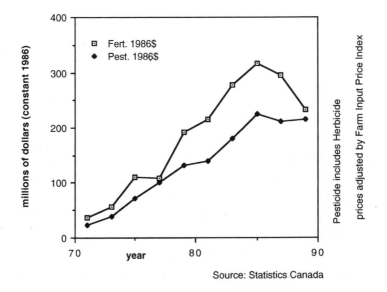

Source: Statistics Canada

tent of the soil rendering it less able to retain moisture. Consequently, the water table rises, especially on low lying land, bringing the salts to the surface. Salinization "is a problem which usually occurs in small areas of 2 to 25 acres ... but when all of these small occurrences are added together, they total some 5.4 million acres ... in Canada's dryland regions ... Although there are differences of opinion among soil scientists, it appears that Canada's ... salinized soils are being extended at a rate of some 10% yearly."[17]

If the increased use of fertilizer on Canadian farms is dramatic, the increased use of herbicides and pesticides is even more so. In the seven years between 1977 and 1984, pesticide and herbicide use in Canada as a whole doubled from 26,928 tonnes to 54,767 tonnes. As the graph also shows, pesticide and herbicide use in Saskatchewan increased by almost ten times between 1971 and 1989.[18]

The Senate report on Agriculture called for a concerted effort to combat soil erosion by all levels of government. But more than that is required, they said. "The changes which must occur in prairie agricultural practices are nothing short of an 'agricultural revolution'."[19] The revolution they were calling for strikes at the heart of our Western society.

Increased chemical use (fertilizer, herbicides and pesticides) is not only a mask hiding the alarming drop in soil fertility, it is also a symbol of the industrial approach to agriculture. In seeking to solve problems in the international agricultural market, some people want to strengthen the industrial approach. If the market yields low prices, this logic encourages more chemical inputs in order to boost production. It is critical though, to understand that the market system as a whole emerged as a response to the problems generated by industry. Consequently, an industrial approach and a market approach are essentially the same thing.[20]

Although the Senate report gently suggests that the problem may be policies that are having unintended effects, they also conclude that "one of the major drawbacks to soil conservation has been the emphasis on increased production. This has resulted in the creation of policies which have ignored or unintentionally worked against good soil management."[21]

When viewed against the backdrop of the history of agricultural policy, the suggestion of effects being unintended seems less believable. In 1967, the federal Minister of Agriculture commissioned a Task Force to recommend policy for Canadian agriculture in the 1970s. This Task Force identified technological development as "the primary worldwide force causing change …. This trend promised not only to continue indefinitely, they wrote, "but also to accelerate."[22] The Task Force identified not only what might happen in Canadian agriculture but also what should happen. Their model for 1990 included: "decreasing … farm population; fewer family farms; increasing farm size … [and] … constant improvement in quality of management"

In what must strike today's farmers as an ironic note, the report also predicted "rising incomes … [and] fewer government subsidies and support programmes."[23] This is in spite of the fact that they also acknowledged that "growing specialization and investment will make farmers increasingly vulnerable to crop, price and financial hazards."[24]

These changes were designed to achieve the same kind of efficiencies in agriculture that had been achieved in manufacturing because they were both understood to be just different forms of industry. They predicted that by as early as "1980 agriculture — both farming and agribusiness —will be a much more trim, stable, efficient and self-reliant industry than it is at present."[25] The crowning symbol of the transformation was their recommendation that the Department of Agriculture be renamed the Department of Agricultural Industry. "All of its planning and operations for commercial agriculture must be integrated around a central concept of a profit-oriented, self-sustaining industry serving the needs of all its major stakeholders adequately and fairly."[26]

Current government policy has still not come to terms with the contradictions inherent in an industrial approach to agriculture. The UN report identifies industrial agriculture as one of the major threats to the worldwide loss of biological diversity.[27] The doctrine of comparative advantage, first articulated by David Ricardo in the nineteenth century and recently recapitulated by Harvard economist Michael Porter for the Canadian government, requires individual farmers and nations alike to specialize in a few crops so that they can maximize production for an export market. This is the mechanism by which the number of crop species declines along with supporting species and local knowledge.[28] Yet this same UN report also endorsed the principal features of market economy which are central to industrial agriculture. It criticizes attempts to manage farm prices because they "distort" prices — that is, they distort price-setting markets. At the same time they recommend taxes, fees and incentives because they change behaviour. Environmental sustainability is not a matter of morality but self-interest and so the problem is identified as farmers who "have not been forced to take adequate account of the real costs of environmental degradation."[29] The industrial approach and the market approach go hand in hand. In order to respond effectively to the farm crisis we need simultaneously to shelter ourselves from the storm of market forces while we seek an alternative to an industrial approach.

An Ethic of the Land as Community

One person who has tried to find an alternative to the industrial approach to agriculture is Aldo Leopold. Leopold (1887-1948) was an American naturalist, forester and conservationist who is looked to by some as the founder of the modern ecology movement. He is most well-known for a book of essays published one year after his death. *A Sand County Almanac* was published in 1949 and included what became his most well-known essay, "The Land Ethic," originally conceived in 1924.[30] Leopold had just moved to Madison, Wisconsin to become associate director of the Forest Products Laboratory. As he put it, "I found the industrial *motif* of this otherwise admirable institution so little to my liking that I was moved to set down my naturalistic philosophy ..."[31]

The key to Leopold's land ethic is his concept of community and humanity's place in it. Working on the premise that all ethics restrain freedom of action because an individual belongs to a community of interdependent parts, Leopold proposed enlarging "the boundaries of the community to include soils, water, plants, animals, or collectively, the land."[32] The implication of this deceptively simple shift is that humans must change their role from conqueror of the community to citizen. (That sound you hear is William the Conqueror turning in his grave.)

Industry required a market system and the market system required all social relationships to be governed by economic self-interest. From Leopold's point of view "a system of conservation based solely on economic self-interest is hopelessly lopsided. It tends to ignore, and thus eventually eliminate, many elements in the land community that lack commercial value, but that are (as far as we know) essential to its healthy functioning."[33] In an attempt "to supplement and guide the economic relation to land," Leopold suggests the image of a biotic pyramid. "The bottom layer is the soil," he writes, "A plant layer rests on the soil, an insect layer on the plants, a bird and rodent layer on the insects, and so on up through various animal groups to the apex layer, which consists of the larger carnivores."[34] This pyramid is also an energy circuit in so far as the plants absorb energy from the sun which is then circulated throughout the different layers. "Land, then, is not merely soil; it is a fountain of energy flowing through a circuit of soils, plants and animals."[35] Land is a community of life with humans occupying only one of the places at the table.

In Leopold's writing, the notion of land as community is juxtaposed to what he discerns as the prevailing attitude of land as adversary. Indeed he understands the choices facing humanity in quite stark terms: "man the conqueror *versus* man the biotic citizen; ... land the slave and servant *versus* land the collective organism."[36]

Many things could be said about Leopold's essay and many things have been said by others. He was a professional forester, not a professional philosopher or ethicist and professionals in these latter fields would want a more thorough elaboration of his position before they would count themselves persuaded.[37] On the other hand there is something compelling about Leopold's position merely on the face of it. We do tend to treat the land as servant and slave and ourselves as conquerors. We are constantly demanding that the land release more and more of its fertility. We stand over it like Pharaoh over the Israelites constantly demanding more bricks with less straw. In pursuit of this goal we are demanding biological sacrifice in terms of whole species. To move from conqueror to citizen would be a shift worthy of the term revolutionary.

There are also problems with Leopold's position. If we accept a community relationship with the land, are the moral requirements that flow from that relationship obvious? In human community the norms for relationship have changed enormously over time. For example, in medieval Europe, people would have thought of themselves as being in community even though the pattern of those relationships were very hierarchical and substantively unequal. If we are going to be in community with the land, what social relationships are we talking about?

In Christian circles, one of the most common metaphors used is that of stewardship. Humans are thought of as holding the land — the natural world — in trust for God. Following from our creation myth as it is expounded in the book of Genesis, humans have been given dominion not domination over the created world.

> Then God said, "Let us make human beings in our image, after our likeness, to have dominion over the fish in the sea, the birds of the air, the cattle, all wild animals on land, and everything that creeps on the earth."[38]

It is a fiduciary responsibility we hold. We are made in the image of God, to act in God's place. We are to be good stewards of the earth. This image is repeated in the parables attributed to Jesus. A steward is a senior and trusted servant and we are frequently exhorted to be "good and faithful servants" (see for example, Matt 24: 45-51 and Matt 25: 14-30). But while the image of trust is a positive one, the social relation being referred to is essentially one of master and slave. We are being urged to be faithful servants in charge of possessions (things) or in charge of life forms that can't aspire to a position high enough up the hierarchy to qualify as senior servants themselves. This would seem to be exactly opposite to what Leopold was suggesting. He was arguing against an attitude that treated the land as "slave or servant."

This aspect of the Christian tradition seems rarely to be emphasized. As long as we only emphasize our understanding of dominion as meaning "caring for" and stewardship as "a trust relationship" the shadow side of these images as social relations will always be obscured. There is another image still widely used in agricultural circles which exposes the oppressive nature of our relationship to the land more clearly. This image is now coming under increasing criticism. The image I'm referring to is husbandry.

Contradictions in the Community of the Land

Husbandry is used by Aldo Leopold in the positive sense. He criticizes trophy hunters as being too immature to be good husbands and calls for a better appreciation of "husbandry-in-the-wild." What he is trying to convey is the importance of the "art of management" in relation to conservation.[39] But are contemporary management relationships the pattern we want to promote in the community of the land? In this respect, stewardship and husbandry are very similar. Both attempt to communicate patterns of management, faithfulness, trusteeship and hierarchy. Both images lie at the core of what we call patriarchy. The distinguished Canadian ecologist Stan Rowe recognizes this connection when he notes that while the term "husbandry" is becoming old-fashioned, the ideas behind it remain.

> Read the sacred scriptures, study the works of the cultural giants, and an overpowering conclusion emerges. Only two relationships are important: that between Man and God, and that between Man and Man. The Man-Planet relationship is simply not recognized ... As an extension of what was expected in their homes, they projected an inert Nature, a passive Mother Earth, simply there to be *husbanded*. Today of course even husbandry is passé. We manage the resource base optimally.[40]

Some people suggest that patriarchy and husbandry are not accidentally connected. For example, Elizabeth Fisher argues that since patriarchy as a social institution seems to emerge at the same time as the domestication of animals, there must be a link. Perhaps the new knowledge of how animals procreate taught men about their own role as well. The conclusion drawn is that the forced mating of animals heralded the forced mating of women — rape.[41]

Others disagree with this analysis. Gerda Lerner argues that Patriarchy began as a functional division of labour and through a series of unanticipated developments turned into a system of oppression. That is, she believes it possible that "the earliest sexual division of labour by which women *chose* occupations compatible with their mothering and child-raising activities were ... acceptable to men and women alike."[42] She cites examples of ancient societies where relatively egalitarian social structures co-existed with animal husbandry as evidence against the conclusions Fisher draws. She suggests rather, that inter-tribal warfare in times of scarcity increased the power of warrior males,[43] that the patterns of organization demanded by grain agriculture reinforced the power of older, knowledgeable males[44] and that the strength required by plow agriculture diminished the power of pregnant and lactating females.[45] She points to the changes in ancient religious iconography when images of the goddess acquire a male consort but the female image is still dominant.[46]

It is not necessary for us to try and settle the argument about how and when patriarchy began. It is only necessary for us to recognize that husbandry understood as trusteeship or optimal management, is a term that reflects a pattern of social relationship that is unequal and oppressive.[47] It is a pattern of relationship that produces violence against the community of women and violence against the community of the land.[48]

The positive dimension of the ancient and biblical view of husbandry is that it was an attempt to express the need for responsible, accountable caring for the community of the land. The negative aspect of husbandry is that this pattern of social relationship, within the context of market society, is experienced by those who are being husbanded as oppressive, demeaning and sometimes violent. It leads to death, not to life. If our current state is that we all live in a market society, and if we still want to practice responsible, accountable caring, our current question must become: what pattern of social relationship can furnish us with an adequate norm or ideal for the community? While some want to suggest an organic metaphor for this task, my own position is that such a metaphor is inadequate as self-description and that we must supplant both mechanical and organic patterns of relationship for a more personal way of being together in the world. This personal approach means that the adequate norm for the community of the land is friendship.

From Mechanism to Organism to Personal Relationship

Stan Rowe is one example of someone who is engaged in an incomplete shift. Rowe has identified our current problems with environmental degradation as the problems associated with an industrial approach to agriculture. The industrial approach to agriculture attempts to solve problems of scarcity through the application of the machine to the land for the sake of maximum production. It is based on a mechanistic view of the world. Rowe contrasts the mechanistic world-view with an ecological or organic world-view. "The organic and ecological view of Nature, as opposed to the mechanistic view," writes Rowe, "is religious in the true meaning of *religion*, to bind together, to make whole of holy."[49] It is this latter world-view that will allow us to "return to the original goal of agriculture and, through it, the redemption of all culture."[50] I take this to be a version of the classically Romantic view which shares in the rich tradition of opposition to the Industrial Revolution of 200 years ago.[51] But because this view has been around a while, we also know that the organic view has its limitations. One person who has thought a great deal about the organic approach is the Scottish philosopher John Macmurray (1890-1976).[52]

Macmurray thought that "every period of human history is the embodiment of a philosophical idea."[53] The period leading up to the Industrial Revolution was a period enthralled by the explanatory power of science which is based fundamentally on the manipulation of abstract symbols we call mathematical thought. According to Macmurray, mathematical thought represents all change as mechanical. That is, the object is thought of as passive and all change has an external cause. Within the mechanism, all change is determined by an external force. From Macmurray's perspective, determinism and mechanism are the same thing. A mechanist approach represents the universe "as a mechanism in which all action is completely determined in accordance with causal laws. If such an interpretation is offered as a philosophy we have what is called 'materialism'."[54]

One limitation of the mechanist approach is that it only applies to things in so far as they are material. Mathematical thought, and therefore science, "arises from our interest in using things" and applies to things only as far as they have utility. "That is why it issues in materialism."[55] That does not mean, however that some things in the world are mechanically determined while others are not. Even this way of thinking, writes Macmurray, is a product of mechanical analysis. "*Everything* in the world is material. It may be that nothing in the world is merely material .... But organisms and persons, whatever more they may be, are certainly material objects."[56] The conclusion Macmurray draws is not that a mechanical approach to the world is invalid but rather that "it is valid for reality *in so far as it is material.*"[57]

To the degree that reality also encompasses the immaterial, a mechanical approach will not be adequate. To the degree that reality is made up of life forms, we need to take a different approach, one Macmurray describes as organic. What differentiates the biological world from the material world are the changes that are consistent within a given life form. These changes we call growth or development.

Development is a process of change that moves an organism from a starting point through predictable and invariable stages to an end point. We can describe this process of change as a series of harmonious differences in so far as the end point which results is the end point intended from the start. We can call this a teleological approach if the telos or end is that which has been intended. So, we can say that the acorn contains within it the telos or end of the mature oak tree. Its oaken future is not a matter of choice on the part of the acorn. Rather we are using intention here in the same way Aristotle used it.

The limitation of this approach is that it cannot be adequate to describe life that is more than organic. Life in so far as it is organic adapts by responding to stimulus. Human life is more than merely organic and while we do respond to stimuli, we are also capable of choosing our own ends, or telos. We are capable of being persons. The organic approach is an improvement over the mechanical approach, but if the community of the land is to include persons, we will need a third approach as well.

According to Macmurray, persons are individual human beings with a capacity for self-reflection which we call both consciousness and reason. People are individuals because while they form groups, they are not completely subsumed by the group. They retain their individual identity. We have the capacity to reflect on other persons and through that, to reflect on ourselves and our own personality. Through reflection we experience that which is like us. We come to know our equal. Macmurray calls this the "consciousness of mutual relationship .... It is this essential mutuality which forms the essence of our experience of persons."[58]

Our capacity for self-reflection is also what we call reason because reason is the capacity for objectivity. By that, Macmurray means that persons have the capacity "to stand in conscious relation to that which is recognized as not ourselves."[59] When two people are consciously relating to each other as persons in terms of their personality, we call that relationship friendship. When two persons are consciously relat-

ing to one another as master and slave, we say that the master is denying the full personhood of the slave. Community can only be personal
to the extent that it approximates the norm of friendship. Complete
rationality, Macmurray suggests, can only be achieved within a
relationship where people are consciously relating to one another *as
persons,* that is to say, as friends. "The key to the nature of ... reason,
lies, then ... in the nature of friendship."[60]

Aldo Leopold identified the primary ecological problem as rooted
in our industrial approach to agriculture. His response was to reframe
our approach to the land. We are no longer dealing with the
manipulation of the material world, we are now dealing with the social relations of a community. However, Leopold employs patriarchal
assumptions to govern the social relationships of the community. It is
precisely the industrial approach to society that has exposed the inadequacy of the patriarchal approach. The social relations of market
society have exposed themselves as violent and degrading to those
without power — whether that means women or animals or soils. The
romantic organicism of Stan Rowe and other ecologists shares
Leopold's anti-industrial approach but is itself limited by treating the
human participants in the community of the land in only their organic
aspect. Since communities are defined by the active relationships of
their members, a personal approach is more adequate for the community of the land. Finally, the moral norm that emerges from a personal approach to community is one of friendship. "Friendship,"
writes Macmurray, "is the essence of morality."[61]

Friendship as a Moral Norm for the Community of the Land

What is significant about friendship as a moral norm is that it
presupposes freedom and describes a mutuality. It presupposes
freedom in that I cannot be forced to be your friend. I must choose this
quality of relationship for myself. I choose it not only because I stand
to gain from it but because I genuinely care for the other person. In

Macmurray's terms, communities are based on "positive personal motivation."[62] Friendship does not require material equality. The parties to the relationship don't have to be the same in all aspects. They do have to be the same, however, at the level of respect. A poor person can be friends with a rich person, a woman with a man, an American with a German, and a sighted person with someone who is blind. The capacity of friendship to overcome difference is an important feature if we are going to apply this personal metaphor to the community of the land.

Some people might argue that we cannot be friends to the land because the soils, plants and animals are not able to be friends in return. This objection does not hold up, however. When we talk about being friends, we are talking about choosing a quality of relationship in so far as we are able. Not sharing the same language will be a limitation on our relationship but it does not mean we cannot be in relationship at all. It doesn't mean we can't be friends. Friendship as a model for the community of the land evokes the same images of caring and respect that both Leopold and Rowe desire. "Agri/culture means the cultivation of fields to produce crops. Within the words *culture* and *cultivation* is *cultus*, to care. Behind it, in turn, is the Sanskrit word *kwei* meaning to dwell with, as well as to care for. We are led back to an idea, deep in the language, that agriculture has to do with people dwelling on the land and caring for it."[63] It also embodies the positive attitudes that Wendell Berry calls for. "To have community," Berry writes, "people don't need a 'community centre' .... Instead they need to love each other, trust each other, and help each other."[64]

Some people will judge the ethics of our agricultural practice not by our duties to the land nor even by our intentions. Rather, they will judge the morality of our practice by its consequences. They will want to know how a morality of friendship within the community of the land would make a difference. A morality of friendship is not a morality of domination. If friends do not support one another they are not friends. When they are in trouble, friends stand in solidarity with one another. They empower one another. A morality of friendship is not indifferent to the loss of biodiversity nor to the destruction of habitat for our neighbours whether they are geese, or deer or worms or farmers. Friendship is typified by caring and compassion — a genuine interest and concern for the well being of the other. A morality of friendship seeks life in abundance for the friend (Gen 1: 28), but it does not worship at the altar of production. A true friend does not promote a life of chemical dependency in order to cope with living. When the community is in trouble, friends come to each other's aid. If our agricultural practice were governed by a morality of friendship today, we would be organizing a massive campaign to redevelop and repopulate the countryside. As Wendell Berry put it, "one of the meanings of our current high rates of soil erosion is that we do not have enough farmers; we have enough farmers to use the land but not enough to use it and protect it at the same time."[65] We would be repopulating not only the human members of the community but all the members of the community. If our friends could speak our language, is this not what they would say to us?

What About the Farmers?

At the beginning of this chapter I reported on my research with farmers involved in farm protest. These farmers felt they were being "taken for granted." They unwittingly expressed the hidden violence of the system when they said "the system is farming the farmers." They experienced not only a crisis of powerlessness but also a crisis of the loss of community.

In relation to the other essays in this volume, these quotations indicate the need to distinguish, yet also to understand the connection between communities and institutions. Farmers experience a loss of power in their ability to affect the forces causing change in their lives. They find themselves no longer being treated as persons but as objects. Others no longer intend their well being. The institutions in which their community was located have either disappeared (like prairie towns), been diminished or transformed (like family farms), or no longer attend to their needs (like governments or co-ops).

But communities do not exist apart from institutions. As Rick Harp and Sonja Embree point out elsewhere in this volume, attempts to build community in a direct and purposeful way have failed. The singularity of the purpose is too narrow and the results can be both exclusive and oppressive. A community of mutual regard arises only as an indirect result of other purposive activities.

While they arise indirectly though, they must be attended to directly. When institutions go through rapid or violent transitions, the communities they shelter are exposed and at risk. Farmers want community — with the land and with others. They can only achieve this moral intention through the purposeful building of new institutions. If these new institutions are to provide for authentic, personal community they must have a radically democratic character. Only this political character will help them overcome the old patterns of environmental, racial and gender domination.[66] Such institutions provide opportunity for renewed community based on the norm of friendship.

Conclusion

Stan Rowe describes the choice before us as a choice between "tinkering" and "transforming."

The tinkerers advocate conservation tillage, meaning such changes as snow management to increase the effectiveness of precipitation, the addition of phosphorous and nitrogen to the soil through formulated fertilizers, the greater use of rotations and leguminous nitrogen-fixing crops and substituting chemical poisoning for mechanical weeding — subtle violence for overt violence — to slow soil deterioration. Such techniques buy time and extend the life of conventional agriculture, but they are not the long-term solution.[67]

> The transformers advocate low-input farming, accenting the organic nature of healthy soil and good food … they judge each agricultural technique according to whether it helps or hinders human participation in the world's renewing processes …. Agro-ecosystems must be designed to meet the expectations of the Ecosphere, the capabilities of the land, and not just those of the people in and on it.[68]

The Senate report has called for a revolution in our agricultural practice. I have tried to show in this chapter that the conditions that give rise to that call have not diminished but have gotten worse. I have also tried to show how it could be that the environmental crisis is one of the many crises that combine to form what we call the farm crisis in Saskatchewan. Finally, I have tried to show that the unity of thought and practice that has produced the environmental crisis, is itself generated out of the contradictory forces of market society. The farmers involved in farm protest have identified powerlessness as a major feature of this form of social organization. They have also linked the survival of the environment to the survival of community in a society with a sustainable economic foundation.

Because I accept Leopold's call for us to recognize our membership in the community of the land, I am calling in turn, for a transformed moral economy structured around new institutions which will allow for the re-establishment of community based on the norms of friendship. Only friendship can serve as an ideal for a responsible, accountable caring that is not degrading or violent. The norm of friendship can generate a policy of repopulation for both organic and human members of the community. It tinkers neither with patriarchy nor with industrial agriculture. It represents a true transformation.

Notes

1. This term was first coined by the English historian E.P. Thompson to describe the moral justification used by eighteenth century farmers to protest the social transformation brought about by the expansion of market forces. See his article "The Moral Economy of the English Crowd in the Eighteenth Century" recently reprinted in his collection of essays entitled *Customs in Common*, New York: The New Press, 1991.

2. A special effort has been made to include the voices of women (through the Saskatchewan Women's Agricultural Network) although subjects have been free to define themselves and some women included themselves during the normal course of events. A special effort was also made to include leaders of the National Farmers Union because even though they were present at the rally, the rally leadership was making a special effort to distance itself from traditional voices of farm protest.

3. Sparrow, Hon. Herbert O., et al., *Soil At Risk, Canada's Eroding Future: A Report on Soil Conservation* by the Standing Committee on Agriculture, Fisheries, and Forestry, to the Senate of Canada. Ottawa: Senate of Canada, 1984, p. 11.

4. World Resources Institute, World Resources 1992-93: A Report by The World Resources Institute in collaboration with The United Nations Environment Programme and The United Nations Development Programme, New York: Oxford University Press, 1992, p. 112, 113.

5. *Soil At Risk*, p. 4, "Old practices and technologies such as summerfallowing and the use of mouldboard plows contribute to salinity and erosion in certain parts of the country."

6. *Soil at Risk*, p. 45.

7. Ibid., p. 110.

8. Ibid., p. 111.

9. Ibid., p. 110.

10. Ibid., p. 108. It is estimated that erosion "by water is approximately … 117 million tonnes [annually, on the Prairies]," p. 111.

11. Ibid., p. 113.

12. John Stewart and Holm Tiessen, "Grasslands into Deserts? in *Planet Under Stress: The Challenge of Global Change,* edited by Constance Mungall and Digby J. McLaren for the Royal Society Of Canada, Toronto: Oxford University Press, 1990. p. 194.

13. *World Resources 1992-93*, p. 274.

14. Ibid., p. 272.

15. Stuart B. Hill, "Ecological and Psychological Prerequisites for the Establishment of Sustainable Prairie Agricultural Communities" in Jerome Martin, ed., *Alternative Futures For Prairie Agricultural Communities*, Edmonton: University of Alberta Dept. of Extension, 1991, p. 213.

16. *Soil At Risk*, p. 117.

17. Ibid., p. 114.

18. Fertilizer use as measured by sales figures increased from $11.5 million in 1971 to $253.3 million in 1989. Pesticide figures include sales of herbicides. These farm chemicals increased from $7.0 million in 1971 to $234 million in sales in 1989. In order to discount the impact of inflation these figures have been multiplied by the Farm Input Price Index giving figures in constant 1986 dollars. The adjusted figures indicate that fertilizer sales increased from an equivalent of $36.7 million to $233.7 million and pesticide and herbicide sales increased from an equivalent of $22.4 million to $216.5 million between 1971 and 1989. Raw data came from Statistics Canada. Calculations were done by the author.

19. *Soil At Risk*, p. 51.

20. See Karl Polanyi, *The Great Transformation*, 1944, Beacon Press edition, Boston, 1957.

21. Sparrow, Hon. Herbert O., et al., p. 17. "Low commodity prices and high input costs have also pushed farmers to continuously increase yields — simply to remain financially afloat."

22. *Canadian Agriculture in the Seventies*, Report of the Federal Task Force on Agriculture, Ottawa: Information Canada, 1969, p. 1.

23. Ibid., p. 8.

24. Ibid., p. 250. It should also be noted that the Task Force anticipated needing to put social supports in place for farm families in poverty and recommended a form of the Guaranteed Annual Income or negative Income Tax. This approach to poverty was being actively debated in government circles at the time but was dropped from the government agenda in the mid 1970s. See p. 425 of the Report.

25. Ibid., p. 263.

26. Ibid., p. 444.

27. *World Resources 1992-93*, p. 130.

28. Ibid., p. 135. See also Michael Porter, *The Competitive Advantage of Nations*, New York: The Free Press, 1990. Following the publication of this book, Porter was hired by the Canadian government to do a study of competitiveness in the Canadian economy.

29. Ibid., p. 108.

30. Aldo Leopold, *A Sand County Almanac*, enlarged edition, New York: Oxford University Press, 1966.

31. Foreword to the 1947 edition of *A Sand County Almanac*, reprinted in *Companion to A Sand County Almanac*, edited by J. Baird Callicott, Madison: University of Wisconsin Press, 1987, p. 285.

32. *A Sand County Almanac*, p. 219.

33. Ibid., p. 229.

34. Ibid., p. 230.

35. Ibid., p. 231.

36. Ibid., p. 238.

37. For a philosopher's defence of Leopold see J. Baird Callicott's "The Conceptual Foundations of the Land Ethic" in *Companion to A Sand County Almanac*.

38. Gen. 1: 26, revised English Bible, Oxford University Press and Cambridge University Press, 1989.

39. Aldo Leopold, "Conservation Esthetic," in *A Sand County Almanac*, p. 267 & 268.

40. Stan Rowe, *Home Place, Essays on Ecology*, Edmonton: NeWest Publishers, 1990, p. 29.

41. See Elizabeth Fisher, *Woman's Creation: Sexual Evolution and the Shaping of Society*, Garden City, N.Y.: Doubleday, 1979.

42. Gerda Lerner, *The Creation of Patriarchy*, New York: Oxford University Press, 1986, p. 42.

43. Ibid., p. 46.

44. Ibid., p. 49.

45. Ibid., p. 51.

46. Ibid., p. 228. "With the establishment of husbandry and the domestication of flocks and herds, however, the function of the male in the process of generation became more apparent and vital as the physiological facts concerning paternity were more clearly understood and recognized. Then the mother-goddess was assigned a male partner, either in the capacity of her son and lover, or of brother and husband. Nevertheless, although he was the begetter of life he occupied a subordinate position to her, being in fact a secondary figure in the cultus." See also Edwin O. James, *The Cult of the Mother-Goddess: An Archaeological and Documentary Study*, London: Thames and Hudson, 1959.

47. For an example of Christian ethical reflection on patriarchy see Elizabeth Schussler Fiorenza "Discipleship and Patriarchy: Early Christian Ethos and Christian Ethics in a Feminist Theological Perspective," in *Women's Conscience: A Reader in Feminist Ethics*, edited by Barbara Hilkert Andolsen, Christine E. Gudorf and Mary D. Pellauer, Minneapolis: Winston Press, 1985.

48. For examples of Christian ethical reflection on the connections between patriarchy and violence against women see Karen Lebacqz "Love Your Enemy: Sex, Power, and Christian Ethics" and Allison Mauel Moore "Moral Agency of Women in a Battered Women's Shelter," both in *The Annual* of the Society for Christian Ethics 1990, Georgetown University Press, Washington D.C. While patriarchy is clearly thousands of years old, some people suggest that it is the Industrial Revolution that really exposes the violent patterns of relationship within patriarchy. See Myriam Miedzian, *Boys Will Be Boys*, New York: Doubleday, 1991 and E. Anthony Rotundo, "Patriarchs and Participants: A Historical Perspective on Fatherhood," in Michael Kaufman, ed. *Beyond Patriarchy*, Toronto: Oxford University Press, 1987.

49. Stan Rowe, *Home Place*, p. 174.

50. Ibid., p. 175.

51. The environmental movement is rooted in a Romantic approach, according to Peter Timmerman. See his "Grounds for Concern: Environmental Ethics in the Face of Global Change" in *Planet Under Stress*, p. 215.

52. John Macmurray is most well-known today for his Gifford Lectures of 1953/54 which were published in two volumes as *The Self As Agent*, London: Faber and Faber, 1956 and *Persons In Relation*, London: Faber and Faber, 1961, though in his own time he had a much wider and popular following. I am turning to Macmurray because of his elaboration of three styles of thought or world-views, which

which he described as mechanical, organic and personal. He elaborated these ideas most fully in his 1936 volume, *Interpreting the Universe,* London: Faber and Faber, 1936.

53.   *Interpreting the Universe,* p. 9.
54.   Ibid., p. 98.
55.   Ibid., p. 100.
56.   Ibid., p. 101, 102.
57.   Ibid., p. 102.
58.   Ibid., p. 126.
59.   Ibid., p. 128.
60.   Ibid., p. 134.
61.   John MacMurray, *Freedom In The Modern World,* London: Faber and Faber, 1968 [1932], p. 209.
62.   *Persons in Relation,* p. 146.
63.   *Home Place,* p. 166.
64.   Wendell Berry, *Home Economics,* San Francisco: North Point Press, 1987, p. 176.
65.   Ibid., p. 164.
66.   A similar point is made by Chantal Mouffe in "Democratic Citizenship and the Political Community" in *Community at Loose Ends,* edited by the Miami Theory Collective, Minneapolis: University of Minnesota Press, 1991.
67.   *Home Place,* p. 183.
68.   Ibid., p. 184.

8

Poverty

Howard Richards

Humanity has paid dearly, is still paying, and will pay more dearly still, for ignoring, despising, deconstructing, and, as Martin Heidegger put it, "destroying," traditional Western metaphysics. Thus spoke the author of the *Summa Theologiae* and the *Summa contra Gentiles*, the two great summaries of Western metaphysics which, just before the dawn of modernity, synthesized the Western tradition, weaving together Greek, Latin, Arabic, Judaic, feudal, and Christian elements. The scholasticism that was epitomized in his *Summae* had been the main target aimed at by the classical authors of modern Western ideology — Ockham, Bacon, Hobbes, Descartes, Locke, Hume, Leibniz, Kant ... Saint Thomas did not exempt the Eastern or the indigenous peoples from his list of victims of the neglect of traditional Western metaphysics; because even though their cultural traditions were not Western, they were ruled today by Western legal and economic concepts which had impoverished their hearts; their minds; and, yes, their bodies also; just as, earlier, modernity had impoverished the common people of its native West. Modern Western legal and economic concepts grew directly from the rejection of Western metaphysics. He did not distinguish modernism from high modernism, nor either of them from postmodernism; nor capitalism from socialism; nor feminism from patriarchy; for him these were all variations on a single theme: disobedience.

Evidently the thoughts the angelic doctor had been thinking, while sitting seven centuries in heaven, watching from a distance the slow disintegration of Christendom, had done nothing to improve his temper. And evidently those thoughts had led him to a point where he was willing to make bold claims, which some might regard as intemperate.

Since the hostess had urged everyone to feel at home and to proceed informally, Frederic Jameson, taking her at her word, volunteered a question, trying to be helpful and to move the conversation along by asking the speaker whether he meant to say that together with the historical process known as pauperization, through which the traditional common lands of the European peasantry were enclosed, and through which the people were deprived of their ancient tenures, thus creating the poverty required by capitalism, a landless laboring class; there was also — perhaps the speaker meant to say — as part and parcel of the same historical process, a cultural pauperization; which consisted, among other things, of a devaluation of the European society's traditional norms for right conduct, which had — according to the view the speaker perhaps had meant to express — protected the poor by making mutual aid obligatory. And perhaps the featured speaker of the evening had meant to say that the traditional metaphysics had been supportive of the traditional norms for right conduct, placing the accepted norms for conduct in the context of a cosmic vision which gave them meaning.

The visiting Saint replied that Mr. Jameson had asked an excellent question, which deserved an excellent answer. Unfortunately, however, he did not think it possible to give an answer at once excellent and brief, and he was afraid that, accustomed as he was to eternal adoration of the divine, he would tire the patience of the company, accustomed as they were to the frenzied pace of earthly life in the present century, by answering Mr. Jameson's very gracious question at the length necessary to do it justice.

After being assured by each and every one of the assembled company that nothing could exhaust their patience, not even a dead man advocating onto-theology, Saint Thomas proceeded to prepare the context for expressing his opinion of the interpretation Frederic Jameson had given of his opening remarks. His words were tape-recorded and the following is an edited transcript of them, into which interpolations have been inserted between brackets such as these: [ ].

* * *

The crux of the matter is obedience to form. Given that value, onto-theology follows.

What I will say will have two parts. First I will develop the idea of obedience to form. Then I will connect the appreciation of form both to today's problem, the poverty and insecurity of the majority of people, and to metaphysics.

Let me say before I begin, in order to allay certain prejudices against me you may have absorbed from the schoolbooks you read as children, that my metaphysical practice (if I may adopt Louis Althusser's word "practice") integrated faith with the most current, the most solid, science of the day. Following my teacher Albertus Magnus, I worked more with Aristotle, and less with Plato and Dionysius, precisely because Aristotle was more down-to-earth, more prosaic. I do not propose in what I shall say this evening to deny a single one of the facts the natural sciences of your century have discovered, nor to contradict a single word that Jacques Derrida has written; now as then my aims are synthesis and integration.

Obedience to Form

The word "form" in modern English consists of four letters. F, O, R, and M. *Forma* in Latin is almost the same.

When I asked a gentleman of your century what came to his mind when he heard the word "form," he said, "Nothing. My mind is a complete blank."

When I asked a lady she said, "a frame for a picture."

Someone else said, "a cookie-cutter."

Another person thought of "a formal," which is to say, a type of gown worn to a dance.

The Germans say *Gestalt*. The Greeks said *morphe*. The French say *forme*, which is pronounced almost like English.

The French contrast *forme* and *fond* (figure and background). The English contrast form and substance.

Mathematicians talk about the "form" of an equation. They contrast formal proofs with informal proofs.

So, you see, I have been visiting different places and times, making myself invisible, overhearing different conversations, and collecting observations about how people use words like "form."

You may wonder why I am talking as I am. You probably expected me to put my discourse in the form (there is that word "form" again!) of scholastic debate, of questions and articles, with objections and answers, just as I did when I wrote the *Summae* in the thirteenth century.

Or you might have expected my thoughts to be expressed in the form (again!) of a commentary on an obscure text by Jean Jacques Rousseau (like Derrida's *Grammatology*), or in the form (!) of a study of Friedrich Nietzsche's writings (like one of Martin Heidegger's accounts of the history of traditional Western metaphysics).

Well, the truth, my friends, is that I am talking as I am because ... No ... It is too soon to tell the truth.

Let me go back to the beginning of my discussion of form and start over.

In certain parts of Spain, the peasants use the word *formal* to refer to a person who does things correctly, the way they ought to be done. To say that people are *gente formal* is to say that they are reliable, that they keep their promises.

I particularly enjoyed my visit to Andalucia, sitting invisibly on bar stools, overhearing the conversations of peasant men as they drank red wine, hearing them praise the *gente formal*, hearing them condemn the *informales*, whom they despised. It was a nostalgia trip for me. It reminded me of old times back in 1250 A.D. I was a mortal then, studying with the monks at European universities where we spoke of "formal causes."

According to us then, everything whatsoever had a formal cause, as well as a material, an efficient, and a final cause. The material cause was what it was made of; its mother, so to speak, its *mater*. Its efficient cause was what moved it, its *vis* — a notion that was elaborated several centuries later by Sir Isaac Newton in his *Principia Mathematica* — a long tale of *vis* from beginning to end. Thus Newton formed (there's that word again!) the world-view of modern times. The third of Aristotle's four causes which we studied back in 1250, inhabiting as we did the world-view of traditional times, as you today inhabit the world-view of modernity, was the final cause. The final cause of anything was its purpose or end, its *fin* as the French and Spanish say.

Now the form, the formal cause. That was the thing's identity, its definition, its shape; it was what marked it off from other things and impressed upon it the characteristics singling it out from unformed matter, from *hyle* as Aristotle put it (*hyle* was the Greek predecessor of the Latin *materia*). The original idea that each thing had four causes was Aristotle's, but we who inhabited Christendom back in the time when Europe was Christendom gave a special twist to it. For us the form of each thing was what it was supposed to be; it was what God intended it to be; the formal cause was the identity of any person or thing because it represented the idea God had in mind before creating it.

That is why I took fond pleasure in listening to peasants talking about *gente formal*. The way they talked implied that the people who are following their form (!) of life (thank you Ludwig Wittgenstein, may you rest in peace) — the form of life prescribed by the culture of the Andalucian peasantry — are people who are living according to the way the world should be; they do things properly; *ils agissent comme il faut, als echte Leute*; they show good form; that is why they are called *formal*.

What I am showing sheds some light, I believe, on why Derrida thinks it important to deconstruct some main ideas of Jean-Jacques Rousseau in his *Grammatology*. Rousseau put Nature in the place of God — this can be seen on almost every page of *Emile*. For Rousseau the way the world should be was the way Nature intended it to be. Rousseau thought he was replacing Christendom's religious metaphysics with a secular one, but he preserved the essentialism we of Christendom so eagerly embraced when he removed God from his throne and put there an imposter, Nature, to rule instead. Rousseau is, consequently, a partisan of Authority, albeit a different Authority, and, therefore, Derrida, always the enemy of specious justifications for illegitimate authority, cannot carry out his project without deconstructing Rousseau's theory of language, and, with it, Rousseau's worship of the Authority of Nature.

But let me go on with what I was trying to say about form. I know you are trying to understand me. Thank you. I mean shape. Order. Obedience. If you will forgive me, then I will forgive you for distrusting my Reality; I know you have so many reasons for distrusting Reality — any Reality. But I am speaking the future. The past is the future. This is not a lie — the past is the only way to the future. Modernity cannot last. Life is not a triumph; it is a slow struggle of pulling yourself together *versus* falling apart. Only grace, whether you know it or not, prevents disintegration from winning. That is what Flannery O'Connor shows in her stories. You should read her. People can't live this negative way; we have to get ready for the positive day. But I digress — I listen to Bob Marley in heaven, and keep hoping that one day I will meet him.

You may be thinking, "the old man's mind is wandering." Perhaps I wander, perhaps I weave ... There ought to be a name for the metaphysics I am doing. Call it "gathering fragments" (following Gramsci). Or call it "running briefly with a stolen word, then dropping it" (following Barthes). Social reality is different from what it was when I wrote the *Summae*. Method follows reality. Back then one *could* write a *Summa*. No, I am not such an egotist that I insist that every word I ever wrote was true. I insist only that you should recognize your loss. That there have been gains in the transition from traditional to modern everyone will admit. The loss. The price paid.

There *was* coherence, not just a utopian dream of what life *would* be like if people understood each other. The beautiful *did* have meaning. Love *was* friendship with God. Now I gather fragments, because that is all I can do, because my method must adhere to reality, to the reality that *is* now. I must be like the alcoholics in their AA meetings, humbly sharing their little stories, making bits of unimportantness beautiful by sharing them with each other. I am just a fat old man talking … I would be 770 years old if I had not become a timeless Philosopher … I weigh almost 300 pounds and I suffer from dandruff. Of course I like to visit the twentieth century now and then to stock up on anti-dandruff shampoo, but I prefer to go home before I suffer from your depression, from your loneliness, from walking your unsafe streets, from listening to you complain about how nobody loves you enough. The truth is — the time has now come, now it is no longer too soon to tell you the truth — the truth is that social reality is constructed by interpreting forms. That is what makes it possible to make a promise, to have a norm, an ideal, a rule, a role, an image of what we should do or not do. Obedience to form is what puts our lives together. If you do not believe me, ask yourself who you would be if you were not a sister, not a brother, not a mother, nor a son, nor a father, if you were … formless!

The empirical evidence in favor of what I am trying to say is overwhelming. It is evident on every hand that human conduct is organized by language, ritual, symbol, story, number …; we become human the same way anything becomes what it is, by form. Our very bodies are structured in their growth by genetic information … again by what I call form. There are millions of good people — everybody knows this — the world around; there have been in every age; I mean the ones who question their impulses. The salt of the earth. They ask whether what they are doing is right. Right for their role. Is this what a proper bookkeeper would do? Am I acting as a parent should? What would a good friend do in this situation? — and then when they intuit what a good friend would do, they pull themselves together and do it; they do that, the right thing, acting as they should. They are the heroines, the heros, the reborn. They keep the world going. I mean the ones who live up to form.

The problem is not lack of evidence; it is that the very definition of what *you* call "empirical evidence" excludes the way I see the world. It does not matter how "down-to-earth" I think I am; it does not matter that practically every page of my *Summae* has practical advice and connects with real-life problems; it does not matter that you can read fifty volumes of your experimental psychology and not find *anything* that will help you to get through one day of life; still, you will always read *me* as "in the air." Am I talking too fast? Is this over your head? You must excuse me if I interpret myself differently. It appears that you and I do not share the same metaphysics; we do not share the same system of interpretation; hence you interpret me differently from the way I interpret myself. Thank you for trying to understand me — I know it's hard. Interpretation, after all, is what metaphysics is all about. "Metaphysics" is a name for a wide intellectual context within which we interpret the many events and phenomena of life.

Your age lacks the capacity to apply constructively the limitless quantities of information you learn in school and store in electronic data banks. In the thirteenth century we knew less, but we synthesized better.

We hit on something true back in 1260 — I am talking about Form as Creator. We hit on something true in spite of our wickedness, in spite of our ignorance, in spite of our physical poverty, in spite of our mental poverty, in spite of our many thoroughly wrong ideas and practices. We hit on … I wanted to say we hit on an important set of facts. But no. It was not the facts; the same facts are there today, but you haven't the language to express them in. We hit on a system of interpretation. It was not really "hit on" either. It grew over the centuries; it was the culmination, the refinement, of the labors of thousands of people whose aim was to make sense of the worlds they lived in.

You too see the facts of form. They are confirmed daily by your social science, your psychology, your natural scientists, your linguists. What is more clear than the fact that human life is ordered? That disorder is pathology? *The New Atlantis* by Francis Bacon, one of the books that created your blindness to reality, was a programme for the future; and what Sir Francis Bacon had to say about using science to improve human life was not wrong — it only needed to be expanded to embrace everything he rejected. A modest adjustment was needed, a mere reconciliation of nonsense and sense, a mere refund of the full price paid for rejecting traditional Western metaphysics. The idols of the tribe, the idols of the theater, the idols of the marketplace ... that's us ... that's the human race ... idol-worshippers one and all ... and I as a Saint can only regret that it is hard to explain to a modern audience — some people do not believe it yet — that Form is our Creator.

Ending Poverty by Social Transformation

There is poverty today because now the slow improvement of customs is stifled by Economics; now when we make some painful progress in co-operating and sharing, in the soft and careful nurturing of relationships, they are borne down, as by gravity, by the harsh demands of the marketplace, and by the heavy artillery of Economic Science which provides the intellectual defense of what moderns call "reality." Martin Luther King, Jr., who grew up in black churches, was one of those citizens of your century outside the mainstream of its thought; he saw history differently: he thought that God acted in history through the improvement of inner discipline, which made freedom possible by making it workable. However, just a moment

please ... I am feeling lost. I fear that I am losing track of what I
wanted to say; the idea that was forming (!) in my brain is escaping
me ... King, Economics, inner discipline, the slow improvement of
customs, poverty ... Please excuse me while I gather my thoughts.

[Saint Thomas stopped and gathered his thoughts. There was a
murmur throughout the room as people used the break to refill their
beer steins, to chat, and to go to the bathroom. Saint Thomas got up
from his chair, marched his burly frame a few paces, kneeled, crossed
himself, said a Hail Mary in Latin, stood up, marched back to his chair
with his head bowed, and sat down again.]

I am the first to admit that philosophy in many senses is no longer
a feasible enterprise. At the end of the twentieth century educated
people, whether or not they have read Derrida, know philosophy's
(formerly) secret tricks. The ruses philosophers have used to give an
appearance of necessity to conclusions that are arbitrary have been
exposed. "Deconstruction" is as good a name as any for destroying the
history of philosophy by unmasking the deceptions used throughout
the ages to make philosophical concepts appear to be true and important. Its patient textual labours are fueled by a moral passion: the passion to destroy the tyrannies ideas have exercised over women's and
men's minds and bodies. I am the first to renounce nonsense. In the
thirteenth century I was known for insisting on the integration of
faith with the most stringent standards of reason. I have not changed.
What has changed is the credibility of reason. But what you must
know is that not every ideology is tyranny. None of you believe the
following fallacy: most ideologies most of the time have been part and
parcel of the exploitation of the weak by the strong; therefore, when
all ideologies are deconstructed and discredited there will be freedom,
fraternity, and friendship. All of you know that if it were so, utopia
could be achieved by narcotics. Turning off the cerebral cortex by
chemical means would answer all questions. Given that we all agree
that building civilization is harder than that, I ask only that you give
me some credit. In the thirteenth century we made some contributions

to building civilization; if you despise us you will not do the good work you are called to do to rebuild your own failing culture.

Your culture is failing *physically*. Let me not take time now — some other day you can go through the litany of the absurdities of the dismal science, treating all existing markets as "imperfect," regarding economies of scale as a mere exception to the so-called law of supply and demand, externalities as mere exceptions to the theory of choice, theories which imply that unemployment is impossible, etc. — enough of that. Let us ask instead what we would do and think if we were serious about ending poverty.

If we were serious about ending poverty on this planet, if we were serious as Gandhi and King were serious, as René Dumont and Frances Moore Lappé are serious, as E.F. Schumacher was serious, if we really wanted to meet basic human needs, then we would be building solidarity from the grassroots up, person by person, family by family, community by community. Democratic control of resources. Commitment. Building consensus. Empowerment. The strength of the weak. Participatory planning. Promises that are kept. Not just a new economic model — no, we have had too many of those — but a cultural transformation of the context of economics, a re-embedding (thank you Hazel Henderson, thank you Karl Polanyi, thank you Charles Wilber) of economics in culture. In a strong culture, one capable of inspiring co-operation.

Whoever said the weakness of words was the strength of the weak?

Poverty is, as you know, a man-made institution. The ladies will perhaps forgive me for the non-inclusive language, since it would give no honor to women to insist on asserting their complicity in the construction of those institutions through which humanity destroys itself. If we are serious about replacing poverty with sharing — its only logical alternative — then we have to create a world where the members of families and communities care for each other, and support each other. I admit that in the thirteenth century we were poor; but in some ways we were richer than you; permit me to suggest that if we had possessed the capacity for producing goods and services to meet every need that is inherent in the natural science that you possess, then we would not have used that capacity in the disgraceful way that you are using it.

Pardon me, a moment ago I should have said "help God create a world where people support each other" instead of just "create a world where people support each other." I momentarily forgot, even I forgot — that shows how bad it is — that it makes no sense to speak of you or I, or you and I, creating a world. How could we? Worlds are made by widely shared stories that last generation after generation, and such stories are stories about Gods, thank you Northrop Frye; I claim no originality for the thought, and apologize for my absentmindedness in momentarily forgetting it. Communities without poverty would resemble those of the early church, recorded in the *Acts*, thank you Saint Luke; they would be places with lots of trees — I point this out because humans and other animals can't live without plants; there would not be enough oxygen — communities with lots of trees where each gave in proportion to her ability, and goods were shared as every one had need. "Her" ability because for all humanity mothers are the paradigms for giving. I repeat myself because I want to participate in an upward spiral of meaning, in which the unpracticed becomes practiced, the unsayable sayable, because the forms grow and grow stronger as they are repeated; the seed is in the trace, thank you Jacques Derrida; that is why unmaking poverty, making sharing, is about form.

My point is logic-al. You and I are not anybody without the voice that relates us. Listen to the voice in the desert; it speaks through you, it speaks through me. Hello Voice, we are codependent. Fun, isn't it? If practice is guided by form, which it is, then the new practices will be guided by new forms, expressed by new voices. We have John Macmurray to thank for expressing a sort of insight which has been expressed through the centuries in myriad ways, and by me among others, using "relation" in the *metaphore de base*, i.e. the insight expressed in the thought that voices, forms, and practices have a common root: being in relation.

Neither formlessness nor violence is revolution. *La douceur est la seule vraie force.* We cross out Community, as Martin Heidegger crossed out Being, to avoid violence. We write a word under the crossing out to avoid formlessness. Community is a sharing of difference; difference is an identity given by community.

The children are wiser than we, as they care for their dolls. They know that feeding the hungry, giving drink to the thirsty, clothing the naked, attending to the sick … is a game, as is motherhood. It is a game that can be encouraged or discouraged by metaphysics, which is, I have been trying to say, mainly discouraged by the persistent, and futile, anti-metaphysical themes of modernity; persistent because the times, in their corruption, call for it; futile because the destruction of metaphysics is always itself too a system of interpretation, thank you Paul Ricoeur. Why not see our lives as essentially fulfilled in giving? That too would be a seeing, a seeing *as,* and, therefore, an *Auslegung,* an interpretation. After Piaget's contributions to knowledge about knowledge, the metaphysical prejudice that is Ockham's razor (thank you, Mario Bunge), which is only elaborated, not added to, in Michel Foucault's *Archaeology of Knowledge,* in any of its many versions, can only be described as contrary to fact. Relations. We were not wrong in our century to nurture our imaginations with images of the divine mother with the divine child.

I do not want to be known as the sort of person who always says, "I told you so." But I *did* tell you so, and although I was wrong on so many issues that I have lost count, I can still give you a good reason why it is better to celebrate gender equality by letting boys play with dolls than by bringing up girls to be *machos,* and the reason is that all being is participation. I *did* say that every finite thing consists of act (Aristotle's *energeia*), that is, its actuality, its completedness; and act is always together with potency (Aristotle's *dynamis*); that is, the thing's capacity to receive actuality. I *did* write in that time now so long past and so far lost, that every material thing is composed of form (Aristotle's *morphe*), which determines what a thing is, and *materia prima*, the matter (*mater*) which receives the form and individuates it. My century's hylomorphism, the way of seeing that saw form everywhere and matter everywhere, could hardly have chosen a more androgynous principle. We asked of nothing any obedience other than obedience to its own nature, because its own nature is beautiful and good (*kalos te kai agathos*). Admittedly, if I was then aware at all that the "nature" of something is socially constructed; then when I said that substantial form was participation in divine thought, I expressed my awareness in a theological perspective that lent itself to rigidity and consciousness-lowering. But if each creature perfects itself in perfecting the others, as I *did* say, then let us together take the next step and say that perfection itself is defined by sets of norms that change over time. And although we can choose to contribute to making forms of life change for the better, or we can fall into contributing to making social forms change for the worse, living (Being) without them is a choice reality denies us; we improve culture, or we make it worse. *Anomie*, apart from being painful, is not sufficiently generalizable to become an ideal that a human group *could* choose, even if it were silly enough to want to. This *Dasein* business, this business of always being the-one-who-is-questioning, must come to an end somewhere, and so must this speech. Let me summarize: (1) the institutions that will bring an end to poverty will be new institutions, built from and out of the previously and presently existing institutions; (2) they will, therefore, be institutions, (3) i.e. forms of life; (4) i.e. forms; (5) they will function effectively only if we mortals cultivate habits of obedience to form; (6) i.e. if we seek to bring our lives into conformity with the good, the beautiful, and the true.

9

Gilles Deleuze: The Ethics of Difference and the Becoming-Absent of Community

Barend Kiefte

> *It is not easy to think in terms of the event. All the harder since thought itself then becomes an event.*[1]

> *In truth, it is not enough to say, "Long live the multiple" ... The multiple must be made.*[2]

Introduction

I am not aware that Gilles Deleuze ever directly analyzes the absence of community in the manner it is theorized by Georges Bataille, Maurice Blanchot and Jean-Luc Nancy. However, I intend to describe what I call Deleuze's "ontology of difference" and "ethics of difference" (though he does not call them such) in the hope that this will indirectly indicate his contribution to the analysis of the absence of community. He provides a challenging view of ontological and ethical difference which urges the affirmation of multiplicity and plurality that resists totalizing identities on philosophical as well as personal and political levels. He can be considered as addressing the absence of community in terms of difference, whether it is expressed as the unlimited becoming of singularity or de-individualization.

Deleuze's Ontology of Difference

Deleuze's ontology of difference provides an important context for understanding his ethics of difference. Therefore, I will begin with a brief characterization of his notion of ontological difference before I discuss his consideration of the ethical implications and applications of difference.

Deleuze's philosophy can be considered as the dual attempt to think in terms of events and to make thinking an event. He focuses on events in order to define ontological difference. According to him, if difference is the primary characteristic of reality, then the possibility and validity of conceptually representing reality is seriously questioned. In this sense he contributes to the critique of representational thinking which is characteristic of many postmodern theorists, especially French Nietzscheans like Bataille, Blanchot, Foucault and Derrida. Deleuze heralds the critique of representational thinking when he denies the primacy of identity or resemblance and affirms the primacy of difference. He considers difference as the principal characteristic of reality and with respect to the attempt at non-representational thinking about difference he states: "It suffices that the constitutive disparity be judged in itself, not prejudging any previous identity."[3]

Deleuze concedes that thinking in terms of difference without reference to a prior or primordial identity is a difficult task. He criticizes unfruitful attempts to think in terms of difference, most notably Hegelian dialectic. It rests on the principle of identity such that any series of differences is always appropriated into the unity of Absolute Spirit. It does not give a positive account of difference itself since difference is merely the negation of a prior identity which is again negated for a subsequent identity.[4]

However, this does not suggest to Deleuze that thinking of difference is impossible. Deleuze expresses his admiration for philosophers such as Hume and Duns Scotus because they offer more fruitful attempts to think in terms of difference. He interprets Hume as thinking in terms of difference by focusing on conjunctives rather than substantives — "AND" ($x+y+z$ ...) rather than "IS" ($x=x$, $x=-y$) — thereby emphasizing the diversity of external relations and avoiding the totalizing principle of identity.[5] He generally considers empiricism to be a pluralism that is faithful to the multiplicity of reality.[6] He recovers from Duns Scotus the term "haecceitas" or "thisness" in order to elaborate a notion of the singularity of events within networks of distributed intensities.[7] He claims that this medieval term designates individuation without reference to the identity of subjects or objects such that singular events exist as unlimited becoming.[8]

Deleuze also appeals to the notion of assemblages of events to articulate difference as the principal characteristic of reality. He defines reality in terms of assemblages which are relations of events with varying degrees of complexity.[9]

> What is an assemblage? It is a multiplicity which is made up of many heterogenous terms and which establishes liaisons, relations between them ... Thus, the assemblage's only unity is that of co-functioning: it is a symbiosis, a "sympathy."[10]

Deleuze claims that assemblage relations are in constant flux because they themselves are composed of singular events which are in constant flux. Assemblages are never identical to themselves because they always become something other in relation to that with which they come into contact and contagion. Assemblages are units of unlimited becoming.[11]

Deleuze's ontology of difference reaches a transcendental level when he defines events as impersonal and pre-individual singularities. That is, he seeks "an impersonal and pre-individual transcendental field."[12]

> Singularities are the true transcendental events ... Far from being individual or personal, singularities preside over the genesis of individuals and persons; they are distributed in a "potential" which admits neither Self or I, but which

produces them by actualizing or realizing itself ... Only a theory of singular points is capable of transcending the synthesis of the person and the analysis of the individual as these are (or are made) in consciousness ... Only when the world, teaming with anonymous and nomadic, impersonal and pre-individual singularities, opens up, do we tread at last on the field of the transcendental.[13]

Deleuze does not define transcendence with recourse to persons and individuals (Self and I) or the consciousness which exists in their depths. Rather, he defines it in terms of anonymous singular points on a surface. For him, the "transcendental field" is a surface of singularities which are more primordial than persons or individuals because they are precisely the conditions of possibility for persons and individuals.[14]

According to Deleuze, events are singularities which are at once immanently and transcendentally self-referential. He brings together the notions of transcendence and immanence, often regarded as opposites, in terms of the "process of auto-unification" of events.[15] The auto-unification of events suggests that they are their own thisness-becomings. One need not and should not refer to a principle outside events to account for their emergence because they carry their principle of emergence within themselves. To appeal to such a principle would be to impose an alien and artificial identity on events. It would do violence or injustice to the emergence of events. Deleuze thus considers events as the condition of possibility for themselves.[16]

However, despite Deleuze's intimation that difference is constitutive of reality — the principal characteristic of reality — he warns that difference is not foundational. He refers to difference in Nietzschean terms: "Far from being a new foundation, it engulfs all foundations, it assures a universal breakdown (*effondrement*), but as a joyful and positive event, as an un-founding (*effondement*)."[17] Difference is not a foundation but the displacement and destruction of foundations.

Difference cannot be considered a foundation because it is unlimited becoming that resists identity. Nonetheless, difference is the condition of possibility for the existence of multiplicity and for the thinking of multiplicity.

Deleuze states: "Philosophy is not in a state of external reflection on other domains, but in a state of active and internal alliance with them ..."[18] At issue in his attempt to think in terms of difference is philosophy's ability to consider new ways of thinking the multiplicity of reality. However, he also insists that the manner in which we think transforms that about which we think. Thinking does not represent reality but creates reality. Specifically, thinking difference creates difference. For Deleuze, therefore, philosophy is a practice. The passage from representational thinking to praxial thinking or practice signals the interrelationship of Deleuze's ontology and ethics of difference.

The Interrelationship of Deleuze's Ontology and Ethics

In *Gilles Deleuze: An Apprenticeship in Philosophy* Michael Hardt demonstrates that Deleuze's ontology and ethics of difference are interrelated by describing the manner in which Deleuze produces a Bergson-Nietzsche-Spinoza assemblage. According to Hardt, Deleuze (a) maintains a notion of reality as difference by appealing to Bergson's focus on movement and becoming (b) gives this ontology an ethical cast by appealing to Nietzsche's call to express difference through active affirmation rather than reactive negation and (c) translates this active affirmation of difference in terms of Spinoza's joyful practice.[19]

Hardt thus indicates the interrelationship of Deleuze's ontology and ethics of difference by describing the basic movement in his philosophy. Yet there is movement in both directions, a double movement that resists prioritizing either direction. Seen from the ontological perspective, the movement is directed towards ethics: "The question of the organization or the constitution of the world, however, of the being of becoming, pushes Deleuze to pose these ontological issues in ethical terms ... The only nature available to ontological discourse is an absolutely artificial conception of nature, a hybrid nature, a nature produced in practice."[20] Seen from the ethical perspective, the movement is directed towards ontology: "Joyful practice brings ethics back to ontology — it exploits the producibility or composability of being ... The practice of joy is the construction of ontological assemblages, and thus the active constitution of being."[21]

Deleuze's ontology and ethics of difference are interrelated and call forth each other. Ontology does not just ground ethics because ontology is brought to fruition by ethics. Ethics may require an ontology as a conception of reality and yet ethics folds back onto ontology as a construction of reality. Ontologically, difference is not foundational but fabricated. There is no pre-existing reality of difference because it is created through ethical practice. The joyful practice of affirming difference creates and changes reality as difference.

Deleuze's Ethics of Difference

Deleuze's notion of ethics is based on a Nietzsche-Spinoza assemblage and an account of his ethics of difference must at least acknowledge this crucial point.[22]

In *Nietzsche and Philosophy* Deleuze claims that Nietzsche's primary genealogical task is to determine the particular relation of forces or the particular form of will to power operating in any given cultural phenomenon. He specifically considers Nietzsche as attempting to overcome reactive or passive forces with creative or active forces by overcoming nihilist *ressentiment* through an affirmative and joyful revaluation of values.[23]

In *Expressionism in Philosophy: Spinoza* Deleuze further orients his concern with the expressionism of power. According to him, Spinoza is properly oriented to the questions about the capacity and capability of the body, what a body can undergo and do, how it can receive and respond. He claims that Spinoza considers "an essence as a degree of power" or being as an expression of power.[24]

In *Anti-Oedipus* Deleuze and Guattari posit desire as the primary force of life.[25] They oppose themselves to Freud and Lacan by maintaining that desire is not the response or result of lack because it is itself productive of its subject and its object.[26] Yet in *Dialogues* Deleuze claims that, like an event or haecceity which individuates as a particle in a relation of fluxes without being subject or object, desire also is not indexed to a subject or an object with respect to its origin or destination.[27]

> What we tried to show, on the contrary, was how desire was beyond these personological or objectal co-ordinates … There is only desire in so far as there is deployment of a particular field, propagation of particular fluxes, emission of particular particles. Far from presupposing a subject, desire cannot be attained except at the point where someone is deprived of the power of saying "I." Far from directing itself towards an object, desire can only be reached at the point where someone no longer searches for or grasps an object any more than he grasps himself as subject.[28]

This passage indicates that Deleuze and Guattari consider desire as emerging through the absence of subject and object without claiming there is something missing from desire. Desire is not the expression of a determinate Self for a definite someone or something Other to complete it. Rather, desire is unlimited becoming without identity. Desire as unlimited becoming is nonetheless still something but never one thing.

The absence of subject and object with respect to desire can be likened to the absence of community. Desire emerges in the absence of community in which social identity, if it ever exists, is always created only to be challenged. We are created by desire for ourselves and others which are (still/forever) unknown and perhaps non-existent. This "we" changes, depending on our relationship to ourselves and others, depending on our position in the field and flux of social particles. Desire's origin and destination are uncertain because it circulates in the space of an absent community in order to create a community which never will be fully present. Desire forges a community that remains unformed and unforeseen. Deleuze and Guattari would not encourage the desire for community as a romantic return to a lost paradise. Yet they are utopian only in so far as their community would be one that existed no place in particular.

For Deleuze and Guattari, desire is not pre-established because it arises in a social realm which it creates itself. "Desire is always assembled and fabricated, on a plane of immanence or of composition which must itself be constructed at the same time as desire assembles and fabricates. We do not simply mean that desire is historically determined."[29] Deleuze and Guattari, again against Freud and Lacan, avoid considering desire as an impulse or instinct that produces fantasies by emphasising that desire is a machine that produces reality.[30] Thus they oppose pure psychologism with social materialism:

> There is no such thing as social production as reality on the one hand, and a desiring-production that is mere fantasy on the other ... The truth of the matter is that *social production is purely and simply desiring-production itself under determinate conditions.* We maintain that the social field is immediately invested by desire, that it is the historically determined product of desire, and that libido has no need of any mediation or sublimation, any psychic operation, any transformation, in order to invade and invest the productive forces and the relations of production.[31]

For Deleuze and Guattari, desiring-production is social-production. Desire is never personal or individual, but always social.[32]

According to Deleuze and Guattari, desire is not to be considered as a theatre or stage in which metaphorical dramas of oedipal castration are played out because desiring-production is a factory or workshop in which desiring-machines operate through breaks and flows to create social reality.[33] As Spinoza does with the body and Nietzsche does with the will to power, they claim that desire should not be interpreted but desiring-production should be experimented with to discover what it can do and how it works. For Deleuze, this approach accords with his critique of representational thinking which only reflects reality and his encouragement of practical thinking which creates reality.

Extrapolating from this point and anticipating others, Deleuze's ethics of difference is not so much a matter of (political) representation as it is a matter of (political) production. His aim is not to give voice to particular pre-established social identities but to advocate the unlimited becoming of multiple identities which undermine the notion of social identity itself. The ethics of difference, as a desiring-production and social-production, is a practice involving the simultaneous and continuous production of ourselves and others in a way that challenges the sense of Self and Other. What sort of practice is it?

Foucault claims that, as a book of practical ethics, "*Anti-Oedipus*" is an "*Introduction to the Non-Fascist Life*" because it concerns the "art of living counter to all forms of fascism."[34] For Deleuze and Guattari, the non-fascist ethics of difference is an attempt to envision new ways of freeing social desiring-production from fascistic structures of power. Fascism stunts unlimited becoming. According to them, fascism can reside both in the state and the Self. It is political and personal because it is both consciously applied by external forces and unconsciously adopted by ourselves. It arises whenever we are repressed with a totalizing identity by ourselves and others or whenever we are reactionary with regards to becoming or change with respect to ourselves and others. If identities of gender, sexuality and race (to name a few) become imposed on us or become too precious to us, then they become fascistic. Political fascism evidenced in totalitarian regimes throughout history is an obvious and more easily combatted form of a pervasive and more difficult to resist personal fascism.

In this regard Foucault indicates that "de-individualization" is one of the most important practices of Deleuze's and Guattari's non-fascist ethic of difference:

> What is needed is to "de-individualize" by means of multi-plication and displacement, diverse combinations. The group must not be the organic bond uniting hierarchized individuals, but a constant generator of de-individualiza-tion.[35]

For Deleuze and Guattari, de-individualization is a process of un-limited becoming. They claim that the psychoanalytic notion of sub-jectivity is fascistic because it represses possibilities of desiring-production into a limited range of options. To them, the oedipal model of psychoanalysis confines people within a strict social structure of subjectivity against their desire to become-multiple and become-other. It creates an "I" and a "we" which are neurotically narrow. That is, psychoanalysis says that one must integrate oneself into a par-ticular personality and one must negotiate one's relationships with others in a particular manner. Similar to the notion of singular events described earlier, Deleuze and Guattari offer an alternative notion of subjectivity (if it still can be so called) in which "molar" identities as persons or individuals are comprised of "molecular" assemblages which are impersonal and pre-individual and allow for unlimited be-coming.[36]

Deleuze's and Guattari's advocacy of de-individualization and unlimited becoming is the basis for their curious appeal to schizophrenia. However, it is important to point out that their model is not schizophrenia as an illness diagnosed by psychiatry but schizophrenia as a process of becoming-multiple and becoming-other.[37] Schizophrenia becomes a suffered illness when psychiatry gets a hold of the schizo and represses or redirects its flight from an identity with another identity. While the schizo must escape from an unhealthy self-identity that threatens its destruction, psychiatry only aids this by imposing yet another artificial and alien identity. Psychiatry offers illusory escapes, refuge-prisons. Schizophrenia, as a process or practice, is more successful when the schizo is allowed to pass into various identities unhindered. It does not fall into the trap of illusory integrated personalities. Deleuze's concern with the pluralism of empiricism appears in his notion of the schizo who escapes the logic of identity ($x=x$, $x=y$) into the logic of conjunctions ($x+y+z$ ...) such that "he" or "she" or "it" is not repressed into a unitary subject but produces multiple subjectivities through conjoining diverse elements. Brian Massumi states: "Schizophrenia is a breakaway into the unstable equilibrium of continuing self-invention."[38]

The appeal to schizophrenia by Deleuze and Guattari is a call to the absence of community and a challenge to the presence of identities in society. For them, when community rigidly dictates social identities, it is often a function of fascism, so the absence of community is welcomed. Schizophrenia is a way to resist fascistic structures of power which operate on the principle of identity. By becoming schizophrenic, or becoming-multiple and becoming-other, we disrupt and destroy the social codes of identity. Thus, to Deleuze and Guattari, the absence of community is not something lamentable that befalls us, it is rather a condition to be actively pursued by us. The practice of schizophrenia is one strategy for this pursuit.

With respect to de-individualization in society, Deleuze and Guattari refer to the "body without organs" or "BwO" as that which escapes (above/below) social determination. They consider the manner in which the body is individualized by society, given organs and organized into an organism is such that its capacities, capabilities (reception and response) and functions are all socially determined.

> The organism is not at all the body, the BwO; rather, it is a
> stratum on the BwO, in other words a phenomenon of ac-
> cumulation, coagulation, and sedimentation that, in order
> to extract useful labor from the BwO, imposes upon it
> forms, functions, bonds, dominant and hierarchized or-
> ganizations, organized transcendences ... We are con-
> tinually stratified. But who is this we that is not me, for the
> subject no less than the organism belongs to and depends
> on a stratum? Now we have the answer: the BwO is that
> glacial reality where the alluvions, sedimentations,
> coagulations, foldings and recoilings that compose an or-
> ganism — and also a signification and a subject — occur ...
> It is the BwO that is stratified.[39]

The body without organs is distinguished into separate organs
such as eyes, mouth, hands, and genitals and each receives their
proper function from social coding. Deleuze and Guattari refer to
this as the process of signification and subjectification because it is
the process in which the indeterminate body without organs becomes an individually ordered organism or a stratified signifying
subject. When they ask about "this we that is not me" they answer
with reference to the manner in which we are organized into identities which are not ours but society's. That is, "me" becomes a "we"
by becoming a signifying subject. By learning a language I take on a
social identity, by making the appropriate sounds and gestures with
my body I am understood as a social identity. Society operates on the
basis of the logic of identity by demanding that we live within the
limits of meaning without contradiction. We must be eminently perceptible and interpretable. We may have secrets, but these must be
knowable if not already known.

However, according to Deleuze and Guattari, the body without organs resists social identity formation. The attempt to become a body
without organs (again/finally) is the attempt to resist individual or-

ganization or the process of signification and subjectification. This kind of de-individualization involves a certain amount of self-destruction.

> You invent self-destructions that have nothing to do with the death drive. Dismantling the organism has never meant killing yourself, but rather opening the body to connections that presuppose an entire assemblage, circuits, conjunctions, levels and thresholds, passages and distributions of intensity, and territories and deterritorializations measured with the craft of a surveyor. Actually, dismantling the organism is no more difficult than dismantling the other two strata, significance and subjectification. Significance clings to the soul just as the organism clings to the body, and it is not easy to get rid of either. And how can we unhook ourselves from the points of subjectification that secure us, nail us down to a dominant reality? Tearing the conscious away from the subject to make it a means of exploration, tearing the unconscious away from the significance and interpretation in order to make it a veritable production: this is assuredly no more or less difficult than tearing the body away from the organism.[40]

What is self-destructed in this case is the social identity that has been forced onto or taken up by the body without organs — the "we" that overcodes each one of us. The body without organs is an irreducible singular event that resists any particular social identity. It is desire as unlimited becoming, the desire to become-multiple and become-other with regards to social identity, the desire to become-imperceptible and become-uninterpretable with respect to social codes. For Deleuze and Guattari, the body without organs is the virtual limit of the infinite possibilities of society. "The socius is not the projection of the body without organs; rather, the body without organs is the limit of the socius, its tangent of deterritorialization, the ultimate residue of a deterritorialized socius ... And doubtless the body without organs haunts all forms of the socius."[41]

This last statement is perhaps Deleuze's and Guattari's clearest articulation in the manner of Bataille, Blanchot and Nancy of the absence of community. The body without organs is the active achievement of the absence of community. By becoming bodies without organs we absent ourselves from the community. That is, we escape the social organization and formation that determines our role in the community. The attempt to achieve the absence of community arises from the awareness that the present community is faulty or false. The body without organs is a basis for another type of community which exists beyond the alien and artificial communities in which we now participate.

Deleuze and Guattari also discuss the deterritorialization of the body without organs specifically in terms of the loss of the face. They consider the face as the process and product of social determination, signification and subjectification, directed at the body without organs. They analyze the face in terms of what they call "the *white wall/black hole* system" in which the white wall is the blank tablet of signification where signs are inscribed and the black hole is the depths of subjectivity where consciousness is lodged.[42] By having faces we exist meaningfully since our face is where we are most perceptible and interpretable. The face is our social identity. Deleuze and Guattari thus consider the face as a political problem rather than a personal problem.

> For black holes on a white wall are in fact a face, a broad face with white cheeks, and pierced with black holes. Now it no longer seems like a face, it is rather the assemblage or the abstract machine which is to produce the face. Suddenly the problem bounces back and it is political: what are the societies, the civilizations, which need to make this machine work, that is, to produce, to "overcode" the whole

body and head with the face, and to what end. It is not obvious, the beloved's face, the boss's face, the faceification of the physical and social body.[43]

Deleuze and Guattari suggest a means of struggling against this social determination that functions by way of the abstract machine of faciality: "Lose your face."[44] However, they indicate that this struggle against social determination should not be absolutely self-destructive. We need the identity of the face to some extent if we are to struggle effectively since the effect of senselessness and self-destruction can only be realized within the context of signification and subjectification.[45]

For Deleuze and Guattari, the displacement and destruction of the face or the abstract machine of faciality which operates through the principle of identity is another practice of de-individualization in the non-fascist ethic of difference. The loss of the face, a personal and political practice of becoming-imperceptible and becoming-uninterpretable, is also an aspect of the absence of community which they address.[46]

Foucault claims that another practice of Deleuze's and Guattari's non-fascist ethics of difference is their warning about becoming "enamoured of power."[47] His claim may seem contradictory, given that they are concerned with resistances against fascistic power, but there is no contradiction with respect to their notion of power as relations of forces. They do not encourage wielding power as a weapon because power does not exist in such a substantial and sustained form. Instead, they encourage applying power as a makeshift tool for transforming the relations of forces. They avoid being sedentary and employing only one strategy of resistance by advocating becoming nomadic and moving among many strategies of resistance. What Deleuze and Guattari seek to accomplish is the impossibility of being identified in order to make it impossible for resistance to be co-opted by the system being resisted. This is a process in which becoming-multiple and becoming-other necessarily involves becoming-imperceptible and becoming-uninterpretable. For them, not becoming enamoured of

power means becoming able to relinquish an identity when it
threatens to codify the subtlety and suppleness of a strategy of resistance.

However, Deleuze and Guattari claim that identity is a function of
power which is inescapable to some degree nonetheless. For them,
personal or political identities cannot be rejected outright because
they always exist through power relations and they must not be
rejected outright because they are the basis of effective entry into
power relations.

> You have to keep enough of the organism for it to reform
> each dawn; and you have to keep small supplies of sig-
> nificance and subjectification, if only to turn them against
> their own systems when the circumstances demand it,
> when things, persons, even situations, force you to; and
> you have to keep small rations of subjectivity in sufficient
> quantity to enable you to respond to the dominant reality.[48]

For Deleuze and Guattari, de-individualization can never and should
never be complete self-destruction. The identities that we adopt and
alter must be as fluid as possible since their fluidity is a condition of
their strength as strategies for change.

According to Deleuze and Guattari, given that identity as a function of power is somewhat inescapable, the attempt to undermine
identity from its inside is evidence of the avoidance of becoming
enamoured of power. Our identity is the code of our position in the
power relations. We must scramble the system of encoding itself by
breaking each code from within. This is the task of de-individualization which seeks to free the unlimited becoming of singularity. Massumi writes:

> The ultimate goal, for Deleuze and Guattari, is neither to
> redefine, misapply, or strategically exaggerate a category,

nor even to invent a new identity. Their aim is to destroy
categorical gridding altogether, to push the apparatus of
identity beyond the threshold of sameness, into singularity.[49]

Massumi claims that Deleuze and Guattari accept the appeal to identities — gender, sexuality, race, class, etc. — as a political strategy for
change only if it is a temporary support to facilitate escape from previous identities or to become something other than what one is already.[50] Yet, if we hold fast to an identity for too long, then our
resistance will be easier to appropriate by the fascistic forces of social
determination or we may run the risk of becoming fascistic towards
ourselves and others who claim that identity as well. Resisting fascism
is not just a matter of resisting external repressions but also a matter of
resisting internal desires to become reactionary rather than revolutionary, either personally or politically. For Deleuze and Guattari, the
ethics of difference attempts to avoid petrifaction in the personal and
political realm by opening spaces for further personal and political becomings.

Deleuze and Guattari would criticize what is often called "identity
politics" because they are critical of strategies which are based solely on
an appeal to some form of identity. In this case, not becoming
enamoured of power is a matter of eschewing and escaping crystallized
identities. While they recognize that we often do speak from certain
identities, they also claim that when we only speak from an identity we
restrict ourselves and our experience. They point out that often our
identities are unjustly forced on us or we take them up as a reactionary
response to previous injustices. Yet both are fascistic forms of identity.
An identity, whether forced on us or taken up by us, never does justice to
our unique experience. The ethics of difference is the practice whereby
the fascistic tendencies of identity politics are resisted.

Deleuze and Guattari are on difficult ground here. It may be the
case that the identity of a subordinated group, however problematic

for its individual members, is the basis of its political effectiveness and its very existence such that the relinquishment of its identity would bring its dissolution and destruction. Yet it may also be the case that the group's reliance on an identity which may have been supplied by the system which they resist signals the group's reliance on the system they seek to resist such that their identity mitigates their strategy of resistance. For Deleuze and Guattari, the strength of a group's strategy rests in its ability to operate without an identity for the most part. However, they claim that subordinated groups are already the farthest on the way to such de-individualization. As far as they are concerned, not becoming enamoured of power by relinquishing identity is a lesson best learned by those groups with the most power and identity in society and it is to those groups that criticism is directed.

Deleuze and Guattari would also consider their advocacy of singularity as distinct from liberal individualism because their position and the liberal position have a different relation to capitalism. According to them, while capitalism appears to be the most liberal (deterritorialized or decoded) form of social organization, nonetheless it is actually the most stringently regulated (axiomatized). To be sure, capitalism affords a great diversity of innovation and idiosyncrasy (schizophrenia), but it is either in service of the system or it is rendered ineffective to the system. Absolute singularity (schizophrenia) would disrupt or destroy the system. Deleuze and Guattari claim that schizophrenia is the limit of capitalism, especially at its outer edges, but it has not reached the condition of absolute schizophrenia which would undermine the system altogether at its centre, as they themselves encourage.[51]

Deleuze and Guattari thus are critical of liberal individualism because it is inextricably linked to capitalism. Liberal individualism, through its relation to capitalism, appears to celebrate singularity but retains the logic of identity. They claim that, similar to the dialectic, liberal individualism allows the unlimited becoming of singularities but appropriates it by relegating it to a particular identity. To them, liberal individualism remains fascistic in so far as it seeks to place a restrictive range on the unlimited becoming of singularities. Liberal individualism and the ethics of difference are not the same, therefore, because the former mitigates difference with identity while the latter fully accounts for difference itself.

In *Anti-Oedipus* and *A Thousand Plateaus* Deleuze and Guattari give many names to the practices of their non-fascistic ethics of difference: schizoanalysis, rhizomatics, nomadology, pragmatics, micro-politics (to name a few). These practices are primarily strategies for resisting the fascistic logic of identity and escaping into becoming-multiple and becoming-other, becoming-imperceptible and becoming-uninterpretable. Each practice is a matter of opening productive possibilities towards an undisclosed horizon. Their ethics of difference explodes, rather than establishes, codes of behaviour. At this level, it is rather indefinite, but it cannot be otherwise.

> It is because no one, not even God, can say in advance whether two borderlines will string together or form a fibre, whether a given multiplicity will or will not cross over into another multiplicity, or even if given heterogeneous elements will enter symbiosis, will form a consistent, or cofunctioning, multiplicity susceptible to transformation ... So experiment.[52]

Despite their Nietzschean experimentalism, Deleuze and Guattari suggest that their ethics of difference is not entirely unprincipled because they provide strategies for resisting political and personal fascisms. Furthermore, to them, the desire that invests itself in society must not be reactionary and paranoiac but revolutionary and schizophrenic.[53] Deleuze and Guattari therefore maintain standards of judgement, criteria, though they are indefinite with respect to what we might expect from political practices.

> Although there is no preformed logical order to becomings
> and multiplicities, there are *criteria*, and the important
> thing is that they not be used after the fact, that they be ap-
> plied in the course of events, that they be sufficient to
> guide us through the dangers.[54]

In this context Massumi writes: "The degree of danger increases
apace with the degree of freedom. There is no invention without a
commensurate dose of instability. All the more reason to make the escape with the utmost sobriety."[55] As with the auto-unification of
events in which events carry their own principle of emergence
within themselves, Deleuze and Guattari claim that unlimited becoming and the principle which guides it into existence emerge
together. There are no pre-determined criteria so it takes great
sobriety to know whether and how to foster or counter the emergent
becoming. We must learn to recognize and resist fascism without becoming fascistic ourselves. The practices involved in the ethics of difference may help us in this task.

However, many questions remain at this point. While Deleuze
and Guattari offer the criteria for "negative" or destructive tasks
such as de-individualization, what "positive" criteria for practice
does their non-fascistic ethic of difference offer? Furthermore,
can/should/need it offer them? They suggest that the attempt to
offer pre-determined criteria for personal and political becomings
falls into fascism writ large because it prescribes definitive modes
and goals of action. Yet we often feel uncomfortable with this indefinite position since it seems to invite all we know of fascism historically, such as the German and Italian states of the 30s and 40s or
the reactionary proposals to cut back on immigration being aired
and accepted in Canada at present.

The absence of community which haunts the desire for community may be considered a call to ethical responsibility for ourselves
and others without the guarantee of a proper response because there

is no certainty about the origin and destination of either the call or the response. Neither ourselves nor others are completely co-present since ourselves and others are always potential or to some extent absent in any actualization. Social identities have never and will never represent the uniqueness of ourselves and others. The absence of community challenges the identity of ourselves and others but it still seeks an ethics adequate to its challenge.

In *The Coming Community*, Giorgio Agamben develops such an ethics in that he seeks to find a way to do justice to difference without falling into the injustice of indifference.[56] He thus further develops the ethics of difference. He appears to be very much influenced by Deleuze's analysis of singularity or "whatever singularity"[57] which he discusses explicitly in terms of ethics and political practice. He asks: "What could be the politics of whatever singularity, that is, of a being whose community is mediated not by any condition of belonging ... nor by the simple absence of conditions ... but by belonging itself?"[58] He responds to his question by referring to the demonstrations in Tiananmen Square as a political event that was not predicated on identity. To him, the demonstrators did not resist the state on the basis of a pre-established identity which held them all in common, but they found themselves belonging in common because of their resistance to the state.

> *The novelty of the coming politics is that it will no longer be a struggle for the conquest or control of the state, but a struggle between the state and the non-state (humanity), an insurmountable disjunction between whatever singularity and the state organization.* This has nothing to do with the simple affirmation of the social in opposition to the state that has found expression in the protest movements of recent years. Whatever singularities cannot form a *societas* because they do not possess any identity to vindicate nor any bond of belonging for which to seek recognition. In the final instance the

state can recognize any claim for identity — even that of a state identity within the state (the recent history of relations between the Sate and terrorism is an eloquent confirmation of this fact). What the state cannot tolerate in any way, however, is that the singularities form a community without affirming an identity, that humans co-belong without any representable condition of belonging (even in the form of a simple presupposition). The state, as Alain Badiou has shown, is not founded on a social bond, of which it would be the expression, but rather on the dissolution, the unbinding it prohibits. For the state, therefore, what is important is never the singularity as such, but only its inclusion in some identity, whatever identity (but the possibility of the *whatever* itself being taken up without an identity is a threat that the state cannot come to terms with).[59]

For Agamben, humanity itself is whatever singularity. We are unique singularities. This is not to say that we never find ourselves in common with others or belonging together with others. Rather, such commonality or belonging together is not pre-established and assented to because it is instead always fabricated in each different case. We must resist forms of commonality and belonging that are predicated on identity. To Agamben, the state represents identity politics in so far as the state requires that even singularities have an identity by which they are given a place in its political organization. He claims that it cannot brook absolute singularity and the commonality or belonging together of singularities which it has not first defined and determined under a previous identity because it wants to remain in control.

I maintain that the ethics of difference and the absence of community that it heralds is required in order to achieve the singular politics of the coming community postulated by Agamben. The practice of non-fascistic de-individualization is a passage to the coming community. The absence of community must be actively pursued if we are to be prepared to receive the coming community. We must absent ourselves from community, which is not the same as an impossible resignation from the *socius* but involves resisting social identities, in order to appreciate new forms of commonality and belonging together as singularities. The absence of community experienced today and the coming community anticipated in the future may be such that we only ever forge temporary communities as schizophrenic nomads in partially deterritorialized spaces.

Notes

1. Gilles Deleuze and Claire Parnet, *Dialogues*, translated by Hugh Tomlinson and Barbara Habberjam, (New York: Columbia University Press, 1987), 66.

2. Gilles Deleuze and Felix Guattari, *A Thousand Plateaus: Capitalism and Schizophrenia, Volume 2*, translated by Brian Massumi, (Minneapolis: University of Minnesota Press, 1987), 6.

3. Gilles Deleuze, *The Logic of Sense*, edited by Constantin V. Boundas, translated by Mark Lester with Charles Stivale, (New York: Columbia University Press, 1990), 262. Furthermore, Nietzsche's claim that representational thinking through concepts is an error with regards to the multiplicity of reality — identity as an "equating of what is unequal" — figures largely in Deleuze's work. See "On Truth and Lies in a Non-Moral Sense" in *Philosophy and Truth: Selections from Nietzsche's Notebooks of the Early 1870s*, Friedrich Nietzsche, edited and translated by Daniel Breazeale, (Atlantic Highlands, N.J.: The Humanities Press International, Inc., 1992), 83.

4. Ibid., p. 260. Deleuze's non-Hegelian and non-dialectical position, which is crucial as a contrast to his positive affirmation of difference, is central to much of his philosophy.

5. Deleuze and Parnet 1987, p. 57.

6. Ibid., p. viii.

7. Ibid., p. 92.

8. Ibid., p. 92f.

9. Deleuze appeals to Whitehead for his notion of assemblage as well as his notion of becoming as events or occurrences which resists the logic of identity. The relation between Deleuze and Whitehead requires further exploration. See *The Fold: Leibniz and the Baroque*, Gilles Deleuze, translated by Tom Conley, (Minneapolis: University of Minnesota Press, 1993), especially 76-82. See also *Process and Reality, Corrected Edition*, Alfred North Whitehead, edited by David Ray Griffin and Donald W. Sherburne, (New York: The Free Press, 1978) and *Modes of Thought*, Alfred North Whitehead, (New York: The Free Press, 1968).

10. Deleuze and Parnet 1987, p. 69.

11. Ibid., pp. 69-73.

12. Deleuze 1990, p. 102.

13. Ibid., pp. 102-103.

14. Deleuze's distinction between impersonal or pre-individual events and persons or individuals is parallel to the distinction between the "molecular" particles of people or societies and the "molar" identities of people or societies which her develops with Guattari in *Anti-Oedipus* and *A Thousand Plateaus*.

15. Deleuze 1990, p. 102.

16. Deleuze's notion of the auto-unification of events is similar to Heidegger's notion of *Ereignis* defined as "Event" or "Event of Appropriation" or that which makes occurrences possible. See *On Time and Being*, Martin Heidegger, translated by Joan Stambaugh, (New York: Harper & Row, Publishers, Inc., 1972).

17. Deleuze 1990, p. 263.

18. Gilles Deleuze, *Cinema I: The Movement-Image*, translated by Hugh Tomlinson and Barbara Habberjam, (Minneapolis: University of Minnesota Press, 1986), xi.

19. Michael Hardt, *Gilles Deleuze: An Apprenticeship in Philosophy*, (Minneapolis: University of Minnesota Press, 1993.)

20. Hardt 1993, pp. xiii-xiv.

21. Ibid., p. 119.

22. Constantin Boundas calls attention to this assemblage, particularly in terms of the Spinoza-Nietzsche conception of joy. See "Gilles Deleuze's Joyful Encounters" in *Joyful Wisdom: A Postmodern Ethics of Joy*, edited by M. Zlomislic et al., (St. Catherine's: Joyful Wisdom Press, 1991) and "Gilles Deleuze: The Ethics of the Event" in *Joyful Wisdom: Sorrow and an Ethics of Joy*, edited by David Goicoechea et al., (St. Catherine's: Thought House, 1992).

23. Gilles Deleuze, *Nietzsche and Philosophy*, translated by Hugh Tomlinson, (New York: Columbia University Press, 1983), 9-10. Deleuze opens his reflections on Nietzsche's notion of active and reactive forces with reference to Spinoza. This becomes the basis of his later consideration of Spinoza in terms of the relation between the becoming-reactive and becoming-active of forces.

24. Gilles Deleuze, *Expressionism in Philosophy: Spinoza*, translated by Martin Joughin, (New York: Zone Books, 1990), 217-218. Deleuze later returns to these themes in terms of the multiplicity of individuals. For example, see the two sections titled "Memories of a Spinozist" in *A Thousand Plateaus*, 253-260. See also the references to Spinoza in *Dialogues*, especially 25, 32, 59-62.

25. Gilles Deleuze and Felix Guattari, *Anti-Oedipus: Capitalism and Schizophrenia, Volume 1*, translated by Robert Hurley, Mark Seem and Helen R. Lane, (Minneapolis: University of Minnesota Press, 1983), 26.

26. Deleuze and Guattari 1983, p. 26.

27. Deleuze and Parnet 1987, p. 92.

28. Ibid., p. 88.

29. Ibid., p. 103.

30. Ibid., p. 96.

31. Deleuze and Guattari 1983, p. 28-29.

32. Ibid., p. 30.

33. Ibid., p. 55.

34. Ibid., p. xiii. This can also be considered as a reference to Foucault's own work in *The History of Sexuality* in which he considers ethics as an "aesthetics of existence" or "practice of the self" over and above a code of rules. See *The Use of Pleasure: The History of Sexuality, Volume 2*, Michel Foucault, translated by Robert Hurley, (New York: Random House, Inc., 1990), 3-32.

35. Ibid., p. xiv.

36. Ibid., p. 55.

37. Ibid., p. 35.

38. Brian Massumi, *A User's Guide to Capitalism and Schizophrenia: Deviations from Deleuze and Guattari*, (Cambridge, Massachusetts: The MIT Press, 1992), 92.

39. Deleuze and Guattari 1987, p. 159.

40. Ibid., p. 160.

41. Deleuze and Guattari 1983, p. 281.

42. Deleuze and Guattari 1987, p. 167.

43. Deleuze and Parnet 1987, pp. 17-18. That the face Deleuze and Guattari describe is white adds force to their analysis of signification and subjectification in fascistic society since being white is considered the most powerful identity in many forms of fascism. Those who are white (as well as male and heterosexual) have more to lose and have to lose more in order to de-individualize themselves.

44. Ibid., p. 47.

45. Deleuze and Guattari 1987, p. 189.

46. Deleuze's and Guattari's call for the loss of the face opposes them to Levinas's analysis of the face as the ethical irreducibility of the Other. Deleuze and Guattari consider the face as the sign of sameness, whereas Levinas considers the face as a sign of alterity. See Emmanuel Levinas, *Totality and Infinity: An Essay on Exteriority*, translated by Alphonso Lingis, (Pittsburgh: Duquesne University Press, 1969).

47. Deleuze and Guattari 1983, p. xiv.

48. Deleuze and Guattari 1987, p. 160.

49. Massumi 1992, p. 88.

50. Ibid., p. 88.

51. Deleuze and Guattari 1983, p. 246.

52. Deleuze and Guattari 1987, pp. 250-251.

53. Deleuze and Guattari 1983, pp. 281, 340-341.

54. Deleuze and Guattari 1987, p. 251.
55. Massumi 1992, p. 85.
56. Giogio Agamben, *The Coming Community*, translated by Michael Hardt, (Minneapolis: University of Minnesota Press, 1993).
57. Ibid., p. 1.
58. Ibid., p. 84.
59. Ibid., pp. 84, 85.

10

Deconstructing Privilege: Reflecting on Audre Lorde and Gayatri Chakravorty Spivak

Eleanor M. Godway

The Master's tools will never dismantle the Master's house.

Audre Lorde

My project is the careful project of unlearning our privilege as our loss.

Gayatri Chakravorty Spivak

The history of philosophy saw the emergence of the ideal of rationality, at its peak in the eighteenth century, in the era known as the Enlightenment. According to this ideal, knowledge was sought by a detached impartial observer who could recognize universal and objective truth, and articulate it in a way that transcended the contingent particularities of his [*sic*] situation. There was supposed to be an underlying rational essence in all human beings — a doctrine we can see explicated in the First and Second Critiques of Kant. This was taken as grounds for the emancipation of women by Mary Wollstonecraft, and it lies behind the liberal stance favoured by some feminists. If it is assumed that women also participate in the rational essence, then the American Constitution, inspired by John Locke, could be a solution to problems faced by women in the U.S. — when corrected by the Equal Rights Amendment. But what all this implied was a norm for humanity, namely the universal subject: "universal reason" specified what that subject would recognize as true and would value as good. The rational human being was the same across

all cultures and all times; as an ideal it would transcend the "limitation" of colour, sex or ethnic origin. Because of this, knowledge can
claim "objectivity," which depends on the subject being detached from
its object, allowing for a picture of knowledge as domination, with the
ideal of a knower uncontaminated by any relationship with what is
known.[1]

To the extent that this conception underlies women's quest for
equality, we are caught up in trying to use the Master's tools. Audre
Lorde was a Black feminist lesbian poet who lived in the U.S. Her
remark occurs in the context of describing the "Master's" reaction to
difference as the source of trouble.[2] Because differences give rise to
distrust and hostility, they need to be mediated by an authority which
all can recognize. It is both the confidence with which we have identified such a universal "point of view," and the willingness to acknowledge its authority — indeed be judged by it — that are currently
being called into question.

In fact, postmodernism has disrupted this version of an ideal subject. It has finally been recognized that this supposedly universal
point of view does in fact have a time, place, and gender — and actually belongs to the leisured white European male. In other words, it
is *not* universal, and what purported to be objective was not, after all.
Objectivity meant not letting your subjective preconceptions get in
the way of your examination of the object in front of you — and I
don't mean to imply this is not a worthwhile goal. The problem arises
when you assume that you can, at will, completely transcend the
limitations of your point of view, and at the same time detach yourself
from any relationship to the object. If, in a particular case, you come to
believe that you have done this, you will imagine that all aspects of
your subjectivity are irrelevant, and that the object is revealed as what
it is. Thus, in focusing on the object, the subject is hidden from itself
and cannot take account of its contribution to the moment of consciousness. If I call this a position of privilege, it is one of which the
subject is unaware. (Hence Husserl's description of it as the "natural

attitude" — that is, as taken for granted and consistently distorting what is really going on.) What this paper wishes to address is the link between rationalism and "liberal humanism," identified as the privilege that doesn't know itself as privilege: a kind of bad faith, as it were, endemic in the "natural attitude" of the enlightened egalitarian.

This naive attitude is apparent in many situations of oppression, where privilege has tended to become invisible to the holder of that privilege, especially if the holders form a group. Thus many whites in North America tend to assume that skin colour is irrelevant, because, as far as we are concerned, skin colour has never interfered with our lives, and being oblivious of the privilege it confers, we cannot appreciate its significance in the lives of those who suffer discrimination because of it. When confronted with the social order which has granted us the status we enjoy without thinking, we can deny being racist because we are unaware of the role of race in their lives. As whites, we enjoy benefits which they do not realize are not only denied to blacks, but would not be available to whites if blacks were not exploited and oppressed. This works the same way for other oppressed groups, as well as in the case of the economic imbalance between First and Third World countries.[3] To be accused of racism can seem unfair because it is not conscious, and yet our claim not to be rests on our being "colour-blind" which in itself ignores the whole problem. It is a case of denying that we have a point of view; at some level it is ignored that we have an investment in seeing the situation as "natural." The same dynamic is at work in sexism. Many men of good will simply do not notice that being a man confers privileges which are denied to most women; some women — this was certainly true of me for a long time — accept that myth of universal reason as sex-blind, as if the way out of oppression is to learn to think like that universal subject — i.e. a privileged European male. (This is yet another way in which power can corrupt.)

The deconstruction of the subject which is associated with Derrida and other postmodern thinkers is not a wilful attack on the values associated with human responsibility and concern for objective truth, but a recognition that the conception of Man as autonomous and rational was indeed a myth. We never *had* objective truth. If one has embodied that myth, and has not seen oneself as an expression of the momentary intersection of historical, cultural and psychological forces which have given one an identity which is only contingently one's own, it would be alarming to feel it challenged. What is at risk however in this precious identity is privilege. Gayatri Chakravorty Spivak has a particular concern with this privilege. She was born in India, into a Brahmin family, raised in an environment strongly influenced by classical British values; a colonial with social, cultural and intellectual status. She once said in an interview:

> Where I was brought up — when I first read Derrida I didn't know who he was, I was very interested to see he was actually dismantling the philosophical tradition from *inside* rather than from *outside*, because of course we were brought up in an education system in India where the name of the hero of that philosophical system was the universal human being, and we were taught that if we could begin to approach an internalization of that universal human, then we would be human.[4]

My excitement about Spivak is related to my own background — an elitist education in England and my own ambivalent relation to privilege, as well as my conviction that postmodernism reveals the flaws in the traditional conceptions of epistemology. Gayatri Spivak herself is an Asian woman, and so on one level in a marginal position. But she is now an established scholar, famous throughout the world, with the prestige of having translated Derrida, an expert and original interpreter of deconstruction, fluent in half a dozen languages at least, esteemed professor and brilliant writer of highly academic prose. And she says, "My project is the careful project of unlearning our privilege as our loss."[5] I like this as an illustration of deconstruction, because it begins to break the rules in the way Derrida does. He wants to show how what you say cannot just mean the one thing you want it to mean. Language itself involves grammar, subject, verb, object establishing an implicitly privileged point of view built into the structure. When we give up the notion of the authoritative reading, the most apparently straightforward speech can be shown to be, after all, polysemic — and readable in many, even contradictory ways. (And his readings can seem bizarre, even perverse, but if they are admittedly "misreadings," they are certainly creative and usually illuminating.) One of Derrida's gifts is to write in such a way that no reading is automatically privileged, and his sentences, as it were, deconstruct themselves as you read them. They are not meant to make sense in a straightforward way, their multiple meanings compete with each other. I think this is true of Spivak's sentence here.

"Un-learn privilege." Many of us who are privileged have yet to come to the point of seeing that we are. In that we have more than enough to eat, a decent place to live, are white and/or male, while others do not/are not, we are effectively beneficiaries of a private law (*lex privata*), a system which is therefore arbitrary and unjustified. But to recognize this entails the loss of a sense of being in the right (rational?), which the Enlightenment seemed to promise. And while we may have been conditioned to think that we deserve it, at this point it becomes clear that the privilege has been *learned*, not earned; nor is it part of the natural order (or the divine, for that matter). When Spivak says that if you reverse the direction of a binary opposition you uncover the violence,[6] she is referring to the fact that in many paired terms, one is privileged, or carries the positive charge, and the other the negative, (as in the traditional categories which always implied that while one was good its contrary was evil, as in the Pythagorean table of opposites for example.) If we "reverse the direction" in the following pairs, and imagine the one usually dominant as subordinate I think we can get a sense of what she means: female/male, black/white, feeling/thought, body/mind, and also as I would argue, object/subject.[7] It can seem as though the natural order were being overturned and we feel threatened and disoriented. I believe this is the case even when it is not apparent that the current weight of privilege benefits us, because, as I implied above, if we could learn to identify with the "naturally dominant" pole, it seemed we might be able to transcend the limitations of the particularity which would cause us to be on the wrong end. (Thus women or "minorities" who want to be included on the liberal agenda may still be entrenching the privilege of the white men.) The problem is, of course, that there can only be domination in relation to the subordinate —there must be losers if there are to be winners.

However, when we have uncovered the violence, the hostility in the master-slave dialectic, belied by the assumption of rational clarity ("objective" justice), can be recognized. And once the struggle becomes explicit, we can feel the conflict of interest, the threat against which we were protected by the defense of imagining ourselves above it all. But then, when the violence in the social and cultural order is demystified, the "patience and pain and work of the negative," as Hegel describes it, can be set in motion. Privilege *as* privilege is based on the exclusion of others. One thing Spivak's phrase suggests is that others' loss is also *our* loss. Having resources denied to others damages us, because we do not exist in isolation: humanity cannot escape "being-in-common."[8] Part of what may change is subjectivity as *ours*, as distinct from *theirs*: if some of us are hurting, then we are hurting. Indeed, we may all be in this together, and who and what we are/have may be up for grabs. Identity as subject claims privilege. Suppose then we have been shown that we are privileged, and at a cost to others: it may be recognized not so much with a sense of loss, as a feeling of guilt. A sort of helpless guilt because we see ourselves as responsible and even know that anger against us is justified. Where this is the fuel for "liberal politics," it is still a cover for the perpetuation of privilege. (Here one might begin to speculate on relationships between Calvinism and colonialism ... as guilt is one mark of the elect.)[9]

In the face of anger we can see is justified, we really know it does no good to say *"mea culpa."* In her essay, "The Uses of Anger," Audre Lorde writes:

> Guilt is not a response to anger; it is a response to one's own actions or lack of action. If it leads to change, then it can be useful, since it is then no longer guilt but the beginning of knowledge. Yet all too often, guilt is just another name for impotence, for defensiveness destructive of communication; it becomes a device to protect ignorance and the continuation of things the way they are, the ultimate protection for changelessness.[10]

The beginning of knowledge? Not the knowledge I was discussing earlier, in which the subject's detached intellectual consciousness assumed the position of privilege. Lorde's comments on that tradition:

> The white fathers told us: I think, therefore I am. The Black Mother within each of us — the poet — whispers in our dreams: I feel, therefore I can be free ... Feelings were expected to kneel to thought as women were expected to kneel to men.[11]

The recovery of women's experience, the experience of all the oppressed, of their freedom, their feelings, their consciousness, spells the disruption of the old values and norms. And the vision implicit in those feelings, the vision of the poet, is not the master's aspiration to domination. We who have privilege — and Lorde saw herself as privileged in relation to many — must recognize it, be aware of what we do have, but we have to un-learn what we would otherwise collude with in being co-opted by that privilege — *feel* it as loss, as a barrier — so that guilt can lead to change, and then it is the beginning of knowledge. Knowledge of oneself-in-relation-to-others, not that which separates us from something to be inspected, controlled and dominated, because at bottom we fear it. At this level we need to trust the feeling which can answer the fear, not suppress it and submit our intuitive response to "rational" standards taken over from that universal norm.

Speaking of feelings, I want now to refer to an essay by Lorde called "The Uses of the Erotic: the Erotic as Power." The "erotic," for her is not primarily sexual, but it is the deepest sense of energy, joy, empowerment, a life-giving source of connection. I think it is what some French thinkers, especially the feminists, mean by *jouissance*. Lorde notes that in our culture this power is feared and resented, relegated to the bedroom (when it is recognized at all) because it is so threatening to the status quo. Recovery of this realm of Being — untamed by logical categories — is frightening because it is wild,[12] that is, under no-one's control. As a Black woman in the U.S., Lorde's witness to it included her sense of its darkness, of that which has been rejected and cast aside, but yet holds the possibility of redemption. She said:

> We must never close our eyes to the terror, the chaos which is Black, which is creative which is female which is rejected which is messy which is sinister ... smelly, erotic, confused, upsetting ....[13]

This realm is of course the dark continent, and even allusion to it has been seen as taboo or disgusting. But its darkness is that of the womb, the source of life, and it is an appropriate contrast to the image of the Enlightenment as a flat space, seen without shadows, without depth or variation or change, or perspective. In a word, sterile, dead.

This chaos is the place where all the voices of difference can be heard, because there is not *one* voice which is privileged. We cannot enter it expecting to be right, or even expecting to be trusted because we do not intend any harm to anyone, we are all thrown into the fray, without the resources our "identity" usually gives us. Lorde calls for difference to be noticed, cherished, respected, even when it shows up the side of ourselves, our history we would rather forget. She is a challenge to blacks and whites, lesbians and heterosexuals, women and men, and yes, children and parents,[14] because she does not use any labels to protect herself, to justify herself with any element of borrowed power. Power of this kind is always at others' expense. The secret is not to let oneself be blinded by this but to know, to *feel* it as loss. Whose loss it is to be is the question, and this is the difference between use and abuse. Whose resources are these, that we have thought of as ours?

What now happens to values, to the problem of the conflict of points of view which the Enlightenment hero was to resolve for us? In a word, politics. In this chaotic darkness, where no one is entitled to tell anyone else what to do, what to be, no one is "better" than anyone else, standards are not pre-given. (Notice how the comparison of people as if they were commensurate involves a mathematical image which is inherently distorting, beloved though mathematics has been by philosophers for millennia. Perhaps competition is linked to counting, to private property and other institutions which measure, divide and confuse us.) This being so, how do we make choices, decide what we ought to do? Is everything of the same value as everything else? (Some postmodernists sound like this; some even criticize Spivak for being on one side — namely that of the oppressed — because they argue that she cannot justify any commitment if she is a deconstructionist.) The way I want to come at this is through what Lorde has already implied about the poet, and Derrida's questioning of the boundaries between philosophy and literature.

Philosophers once saw knowledge and truth as their domain, privileging themselves above poetry, fiction etc. This was still the case, even when they began to limit their aspirations to relative versions of truth, or to analysis of concepts. Now, if the boundaries are less clear it might be more honest if they could envisage their work as creative or persuasive in the manner of traditional essayists, expressive of *their* point of view. In any case, there has been a tendency to claim authority, even if they know it cannot be justified. And maybe their talk is no more than rhetoric (as Rorty tends to suggest) in the sense that whatever persuades you, you should go along with, because there is no standard, no test for truth. This surely leaves us open to the bullying of politicians, the naked exercise of power, the resultant oppression.[15]

Audre Lorde's response to this was not to resort to universal moral judgment, but was an exhortation to do "what feels right." And this is not a wishy washy emotional appeal, but on the contrary, it involves a profoundly disciplined feeling which depends on our honestly confronting our deepest fears. This is the true meaning of the education of desire. She explained in her essay "The Transformation of Silence into Language and Action,"[16] as she found herself forced to speak out after she faced the news of her cancer. Being silent had not protected her — but having had to face her deepest fear, she could take new risks. One can feel the cost of this when one reads her poem:

A Litany For Survival

For those of us who live at the shoreline
standing upon the constant edges of decision
crucial and alone
for those of us who cannot indulge
the passing dreams of choice
who love in doorways coming and going
in the hours between dawns
looking inward and outward
at once before and after
seeking a now that can breed
futures

like bread in our children's mouths
so their dreams will not reflect the death of ours;
For those of us
who were imprinted with fear
like a faint line in the center of our foreheads
learning to be afraid with our mother's milk
for by this weapon this
illusion of some safety to be found
the heavy-footed hoped to silence us
For all of us
this instant and this triumph
We were never meant to survive.

And when the sun rises we are afraid
it might not remain
when the sun sets we are afraid
it might not rise in the morning
when our stomachs are full we are afraid of
indigestion
when our stomachs are empty we are afraid
we may never eat again
when we are loved we are afraid
love will vanish
when we are alone we are afraid
love will never return
and when we speak we are afraid
our words will not be heard
nor welcomed but
when we are silent
we are still afraid.
So it is better to speak
remembering
we were never meant to survive.[17]

The crucial distinction to be made here is that between poetry and rhetoric;[18] between words that can "breed futures" in the face of our fears, and words which side with those fears. Poetry, we have glimpsed in the reference to the "Black mother within each of us," but she explains at length in "Poetry is not a Luxury":

> The quality of light by which we scrutinize our lives has direct bearing upon the product which we live, and upon the changes which we hope to bring about through those lives. It is within this light that we form those ideas by which we pursue our magic and make it realized. This is poetry as illumination ...[19]

This light is not that of the Enlightenment, the light from everywhere and nowhere, but it is our light, kindled from within us, experienced also as *jouissance*, which opens up the clearing, as Heidegger describes it, within which truth happens, and I want to say, life is possible because the future is open. The light then, comes out of the darkness of dreaming and feeling, and illumines by bringing those visions into the real world, where changes are made. There are no guarantees here, but there are ways to orient ourselves by listening to different voices and disciplining ourselves to surrender to being changed — to perform something like the phenomenological reduction, in the faith not that there will be a revelation of universal truth, but that we will be open enough to respond from the right place, and there will be what Kurt Wolff calls "the catch."[20]

What is there to protect us from chaotic relativism, the Hitlers and Goebbels and our own evil impulses? Only our own capacity to trust, and the awareness that we must question ourselves, "scrutinize our lives," lest we be the source of betrayal.

Notes

1. Merleau-Ponty called it "High altitude thinking," (*penser de survol*).
2. Audre Lorde, *Sister Outsider,* Crossing Press, 1984, p. 110-113.
3. See *The Post-Colonial Critic,* Gayatri Chakravorty Spivak, Routledge, 1990, p. 96-97.
4. Ibid., p. 7.
5. Ibid., p. 9.
6. Ibid., p. 8.
7. See "Perception and Dialectic," in *Human Studies,* Spring 1979, published under my former name, Eleanor M. Shapiro.
8. In the words of Jean-Luc Nancy. See "Of Being-in-Common," in *Community at Loose Ends,* edited by Miami Theory Collective, University of Minnesota Press, 1991.
9. I owe this suggestion to a remark made by William Burney.
10. Lorde, op. cit., p. 130.
11. Spivak, op. cit., p. 38, 39.
12. Cf. Geraldine Finn's "space-between;" and "wild being" (*être sauvage*) as discussed by Merleau-Ponty — which cannot be appropriated, but is recognized at the moment that it puts us in question. (See my article "Wild being, the prepredicative and expression: how Merleau-Ponty uses phenomenology to develop an ontology," in *Man and World,* No. 26, Fall 1993.
13. Spivak, op. cit., p. 101.
14. See "Man Child ..." *Sister Outsider,* p. 75-76.
15. Is this perhaps the problem for Heidegger, whose recognition of the limitations of rational thought has been so important? Does the most persuasive rhetoric win? And what after all *is* "winning"?
16. Lorde, op. cit., p. 40-44.
17. Audre Lorde, *The Black Unicorn,* W. W. Norton, New York/London, 1978, p. 31f.
18. Cf. Lorde's poem "Power" which begins: "The difference between poetry and rhetoric is being ready to kill yourself instead of your children." (*The Black Unicorn,*) p. 108f. It is about a black woman who was a member of the jury (the rest of whom were white men) which acquitted a white policeman who had killed a ten year old black boy.
19. Lorde, op. cit., p. 36.
20. The linked notions of surrender-and-catch are developed by Kurt Wolff, in *Surrender and Catch,* Dordrecht, Reidel, 1976 (and elsewhere). He describes "surrender" as "an undifferentiated state and relation"; five elements are required for it to happen: total involvement; suspension of received notions; pertinence of everything; identification; and risk of being hurt. (*op. cit.* ch. 4). The "catch" is the unlooked-for effect (yield, transformation, creation), which can come into being as a result of surrender, another name for which is "cognitive love." See my article "Faith *and* Knowledge in Crisis: towards an Epistemology of the Cross," in *Listening, a Journal of Religion and Culture,* Spring 1992, especially, pp. 103-106. ("Surrender and Catch, a Response to Crisis.")

POLITICAL ECOLOGY
Beyond Environmentalism

Dimitrios I. Roussopoulos

Examining the perspective offered by various components of political ecology, this book presents an overview of its origins as well as its social and cultural causes. It summarizes the differences, and similarities, between political ecology and social ecology, while revealing, quite candidly, that the resolution of the present planetary crisis hinges on the outcome and consequences of this new politics.

140 pages, index
Paperback ISBN: 1-895431-80-8 $15.99
Hardcover ISBN: 1-895431-81-6 $34.99
L.C. No. 93-72749

GLOBAL VISIONS
Beyond the New World Order

Jeremy Brecher, John Brown Childs, and Jill Cutler, editors

All over the world, grassroots movements are forging links across national boundaries to resist the New World Order. Their aims are to restore the power of communities to nurture their environments; to enhance the access of ordinary people to the resources they need; and to democratize local, national, and international institutions. Such efforts provide a practical starting point for the construction of a genuine world community. *Global Visions* initiates a crucial worldwide discussion on what such an alternative might be — and on how to create it.

317 pages, index
Paperback ISBN: 1-895431-74-3 $19.99
Hardcover ISBN: 1-895431-75-1 $38.99

THE POLITICS OF INDIVIDUALISM
Liberalism, Liberal Feminism and Anarchism

L. Susan Brown

This work focuses specifically on the similarities and differences of liberal and anarchist political philosophies. The main contribution of this work is its original argument that anarcho-communism and liberalism (and their feminist offshoots) are first and foremost *individualist* in nature, and therefore share certain assumptions and understandings.

198 pages, index
Paperback ISBN: 1-895431-78-6 $19.99
Hardcover ISBN: 1-895431-79-4 $38.99
L.C. No. 93-72750

CULTURE AND SOCIAL CHANGE
Social Movements in Québec and Ontario

Colin Leys and Marguerite Mendell, editors

In contrast with the current tendency to see 'culture' only as an increasingly commodified instrument of social control in the hands of a power elite, the work collected in this volume reveals cultural transformations occurring in the older social movements, such as the labour movement and the churches, and creative new energies being released in the culture of the new social movements such as the women's movement, the ecology movement and community organizations.

230 pages
Paperback ISBN: 1-895431-28-X $19.95
Hardcover ISBN: 1-895431-29-8 $38.95
L.C. No.92-70625

COMMUNITY ECONOMIC DEVELOPMENT
In Search of Empowerment and Alternatives

Eric Shragge, editor

Community Economic Development challenges the notion that the economy is privately owned and controlled, and argues that the economy should both act in the social interest of the local community and be at least partially controlled by it. This book explores the limits and potentials of an important part of a new economics.

141 pages
Paperback ISBN: 1-895431-86-7 $19.99
Hardcover ISBN: 1-895431-87-5 $38.99
ISSN: 1195-1850
L.C. No. 93-72747

This book is part of the School of Social Work, McGill University, monograph series.

CIVILIZATION AND ITS DISCONTENTED

John F. Laffey

1993 QSPELL Award Finalist

The craft of the historian is to study the past and analyze it for present and future generations. Laffey certainly does this.
The Montreal Gazette

In the three extended essays of *Civilization and Its Discontented*, John Laffey explores various notions of civilization and their social uses.

175 pages, index
Paperback ISBN: 1-895431-70-0 $16.99
Hardcover ISBN: 1-895431-71-9 $35.99
L.C. No. 93-70388